KaChing

KaChing

How to Run an Online Business
that Pays and Pays

JOEL COMM

WILEY

John Wiley & Sons, Inc.

Published by John Wiley & Sons, Inc., Hoboken, New Jersey.
Published simultaneously in Canada.

For general information on our other products and services or for technical support, please contact our Customer Care Department within the United States at (800) 762-2974, outside the United States at (317) 572-3993 or fax (317) 572-4002.

Wiley also publishes its books in a variety of electronic formats. Some content that appears in print may not be available in electronic books. For more information about Wiley products, visit our web site at www.wiley.com.

ISBN 978-0-470-59767-5 (cloth); ISBN 978-0-470-64442-3 (ebk); ISBN 978-0-470-64443-0 (ebk); ISBN 978-0-470-64444-7 (ebk)

Printed in the United States of America

10 9 8 7 6 5 4 3 2 1

Contents

Foreword

For the first time in human history, the playing field has been leveled because the Internet makes it possible for each and every one of us to plug in electronically and make money. Whether it's with our own product, as the affiliate of somebody else's product, as an application for products such as the iPhone and the PulsePen, or whatever. Your fortune is waiting in front of you and this book is going to show you how to get from here to there in the smoothest, easiest, most omni-effective way possible.

If you take your passion, your problem, or your pain, you can turn it into profit and you can do it online more elegantly and effectively than any other way in human history because you can do it in the privacy of your own home. If you read my book *The Richest Kids in America,* 80% of them have made absolute fortunes by applying the new electronic media. The new fortune, the 21st century real estate fortune is in the Internet media. It doesn't matter when you come online, it matters *that* you come online, and come into total awareness that this book teaches you how to use it and maximize it to your benefit and the benefit of all those whom you're going to serve.

Each of us has content that we don't even know we have. Thanks to a book called *The Long Tail*, you can pick a very specific niche market and become vastly rich for the first time in human history. It's never been more exciting with companies like Google that make more profit than anybody else and has become the number one brand in the world. In eight years, they've become bigger than Coca-Cola and Campbell's Soup, and you can use the power of everything that Google has to make your product, service, or information sell in multiple ways for multiple pays. We are in the digital age. We've left the information age, come into the digital age, and everyone has got compression and you can go straight from you and your product that you could invent in your mind today, press a button, and have it become money in your immediate tomorrows.

The beautiful thing about the Internet is that you can be the broker. Somebody else has got the market. You have got the people who want to buy it and you take the in-between fee. This book teaches you how to master money-making online, in the sweet now and now.

What you're about to read from my friend Joel Comm is how to have a massive, passive, permanent income online and have it be residual so you get paid again, and again, and again into your future.

You're going to learn all the techniques, tricks, and secrets of how to make yourself the authority figure, with mega credibility, so people will want to throw their cash at you. Get results! You're going to be back in the saddle of high finance again with an awareness that you didn't have before reading this great, grand, and terrific book.

—Mark Victor Hansen
Co-creator, #1 *New York Times* bestselling series
Chicken Soup for the Soul®
Co-author, *Cracking the Millionaire Code*,
The One Minute Millionaire, and *Cash in a Flash*
Author, *Richest Kids in America*

Introduction—Creating Your Personal KaChing Button

When the Internet took off, it introduced a whole bunch of new sounds into our lives. We've grown used to hearing the two-note ring that tells us we have mail. We can recognize the rising sound of Windows opening up across a crowded Starbucks. And we all know the death-knell "bong" warning us that we've just done something wrong.

But there's one sound we don't hear on computers, even though it's been part of our lives for decades: the "KaChing" sound a cash register makes when it opens.

That's a real shame, because to an entrepreneur, there's no music like it.

It's not just the announcement that you're getting money—although that's always very nice. It's the declaration that you've achieved success.

You've made a sale!

You had an idea. You did the research. You created your product, and when you launched it in the marketplace . . . it worked!

You were right!

People *do* like the idea. They like it so much, they're even willing to put their hands in their pockets and give you their own money for it. There's no greater proof of your ability than that.

It's an incredible feeling. Not even your first paycheck can compare to it. There are no risks involved in renting your skills to an employer. There's no investment, so the rewards are much lower, too.

But when you're setting up your own business, when you're launching a product—even if it's a product as simple as an ad-supported web site—you're investing your time, your passion, and yes, perhaps a little of your money, too. It's the biggest test you'll ever take. It's not a test of your knowledge. There are plenty of people around with brains like encyclopedias who are barely making minimum wage. This is a test of your imagination, your creativity, and your ability to get things done.

The stakes are higher, the thrills are higher, and the rewards when it all comes together are so much higher, too.

If you are the owner of a brand-new store opening your doors for the first time, you have no idea whether your dream will fly or whether you're going to be shutting down before you've even had a chance to declare your first end-of-season sale.

But when you open your cash register and hear that Ka-Ching sound for the first time, you know. Even if the business doesn't succeed—and many new businesses don't—you know you've achieved something.

You've taken a business idea from concept through implementation to launch. And you have persuaded someone to buy. You got there.

If you've done that once, you can do it again. And again. And again.

You have what it takes to be a successful entrepreneur, and you're going to be hearing that ring of success for the rest of your life.

But we don't get that on the Internet.

When a check from Google lands in your mailbox, there's no KaChing sound.

When money arrives in your PayPal account, you might hear the sound of an incoming e-mail, but that's not the same as "KaChing."

Maybe that's a good thing. In a bricks-and-mortar business, sales usually come in spurts. People line up, hand over their credit cards or their cash, and process their purchase. Each sale is an event, one that can be celebrated with its own ring.

Online, sales come in all the time. Day and night, weekday and weekend, from Washington, Wisconsin, and Wellington, New Zealand, anyone, anywhere, anytime can push a button on his or her computer and give you money.

And you don't have to do anything. You don't have to stand behind the cash register. You don't have to count the change. You don't even have to smile and wish your customers a nice day.

It's all automated. Set up the system and your online business will practically run itself. All you have to do is cash the checks.

It would be nice to have a KaChing, though.

This book isn't going to make a KaChing sound. It's going to do something even better. It's going to help you create a KaChing system. It's going to explain the principles behind an Internet business that makes money, and it's going to provide real, practical advice to help you build your own.

Those suggestions aren't going to be general ideas about what might work or what should work. They're not going to be theoretical. They're going to be the real strategies that have worked for me.

If you count dialing into local bulletin board systems (BBS) in 1980, I've been online for more than 30 years. I built my first web site in 1995. That might not sound like a long time, but in Internet years, it feels like forever. When I launched my first site, there were only about 25,000 other sites on the Web. In September 2009, Netcraft, an Internet services company, found that the top half dozen or so hosting companies alone were serving an incredible 226,099,841 web sites.

With that growth has come the money. Advertising distributed by the top four online ad agencies—Google, Yahoo!, Microsoft, and AOL—was worth $32.9 billion in 2008. In Britain, more advertising money is now spent on the Web than on television.

And that's just the cash spent persuading people to buy. In 2008, Forrester Research estimated the value of retail sales made online worldwide at more than $200 billion.

That's a fantastic opportunity. It's a gigantic gold mine, and it's one that everyone has access to. You don't need to own a giant media company to take a share of that revenue. You don't need a degree in computing, communications, or advanced nuclear physics to make money online. You just need to know how the system works and have the patience and the drive to succeed.

In the time that I've been online, I've seen all sorts of ways that entrepreneurs can divert the funds flowing on the Internet toward their own cash registers. Not all of them have proved to be as great as promised, but the best ideas have stuck around. They've proven their value to sellers, to buyers, to publishers, and to advertisers.

In this book, I'll describe those methods, and I'll explain how you can make them work for you.

I'll begin by talking about the New Web Order.

The Internet has revolutionized the business environment. It hasn't just created an entirely new way of buying and selling products and services, it has also democratized business.

If once you needed capital, contacts, experience, and an appetite for risk to become an entrepreneur, today you don't need anything more than a computer and an Internet connection. That's a genuine social revolution. It's capitalism for the masses. It's the chance of KaChing for people who don't even own a cash register.

In Chapter 1 I talk about what it means for you and how people like you have been using that new landscape to make a mint.

Then in Chapter 2 I discuss what you need to build an Internet business. You won't find a long equipment list here. Instead, you'll find a discussion of ideas because that's really what you need to succeed online. Understand what you love, recognize your passion, and you'll know your niche. Success will follow. I explain how to do it.

Presenting that passion will usually come by delivering content. It's often been said that content on the Internet is king. I prefer to think of it differently. I like to think of content as *KaChing*. Good content is money, and the better the content, the greater the amounts of money. In Chapter 3 I talk about more than a dozen different ways to turn content into cash.

Content is usually delivered on web sites, but that's not the only way of getting information from you to people willing to pay for it. Another method is through information products sold across the Internet. These can be incredibly powerful and open a whole new opportunity to sell knowledge for its true value. In Chapter 4 I tell you what you need to do create your product line—and sell it.

Information certainly isn't the only kind of commodity you can sell online. Affiliate programs have now become a standard way for savvy marketers to sell anything from cars and computers to books and buzz saws. Just one of my sites alone generates five-figure commissions every single month through affiliate sales. It's simple, and it's certainly rewarding, but you have to find the right products, the right market, and follow the rules. Chapter 5 explains what I do to make the sales.

Affiliate sales should come in a steady flow, but the best kinds of sales are subscriptions. These are guaranteed payments that you can rely on month after month. They can form the basis of a business, giving an entrepreneur a solid foundation on which to grow. They require a little more thought than conventional web sites, but they can be lucrative, valuable, and enjoyable. My membership site has brought in tens of thousands of members who pay $78 per month each. In Chapter 6 I tell you what I do so that you can do the same thing.

And once you're achieving success, you'll find that you've picked up two more assets that are more valuable than anything you'll have sold until now: *knowledge* and *experience*. You can't sell those assets, but you can sell the benefits of those assets. Coaching programs are a fantastic way to give back to the community of entrepreneurs—and make even more money from your achievements. In Chapter 7 I explain how to offer both group and personal coaching, and how to use branding and PR to bring in clients.

Finally, in Chapter 8 I provide a bunch of examples that illustrate many of the strategies that I've described in this book. There's no point in reinventing the wheel when someone's done all the hard work for you. One of the most important steps to success is to build on the achievements of others. When you achieve success, you can be certain that others will be building on your accomplishments, too. You'll be able to use these case studies as models for your own business.

In a bricks-and-mortar store, there's only one way to generate a KaChing sound. It happens when a customer agrees to swap hard-earned cash for the product the store owner has agreed to sell. Online, your opportunity is much, much bigger. There are five primary methods of making money on the Web, and I explain how I use all of them in my multi-million-dollar Internet business.

By the time you've finished reading this book, you'll have all the information you need not just to create a successful online business—that's easy—but to create an online business that makes the most of *all* of the Internet's most powerful revenue-generating opportunities.

That's not a one-off KaChing ring. It's a constant chime that will accompany you as you continue to grow and develop your online business.

Let's start by looking at just what those opportunities can bring.

KaChing

The New Web Order—How the Internet Has Brought Opportunity to Everybody

My first KaChing moment was not a pleasant sound. It was more like a thud than a ring. It wasn't the tinkle of a bell, and it wasn't even the pleasing sound that the cash drawer makes as it opens.

It was the sound of a cardboard box landing on the kitchen table.

But to me it was sweet music.

The year was 1994, and I'd already been playing around with computers—the simplest kind, the type that are less powerful than today's MP3 players—since 1980.

Of course, when I say "playing around" what I actually mean is "playing."

I'd had all the right intentions when I bought my first computer. I'd looked at the manual that explained how to create BASIC code and tried to write a few simple programs. I even got the screen to show "Hello world!" and felt very proud of myself. But I also discovered that to play a game all you had to do was stuff a floppy

1

disk into a slot and wait for the program to load. That was so much easier and so much more fun.

I never did learn programming. In fact, I can't code my way out of a paper bag. I leave that to those who are far more knowledgeable and talented in that arena. However, I have always had a love for computer games.

Games cost money, and back in the mid-1990s, I had the sort of income that meant every penny had its place. My career until then had consisted of a mixture of disc jockeying at weddings and bar mitzvahs and selling encyclopedias door to door. I couldn't really justify feeding my hobby with every new game that came out. That was when I spotted my first computer-related business opportunity.

It happened while I was reading reviews in a computer games magazine. I realized that the reviewers were getting their games for free. They got to play all the new games, and they didn't have to pay for any of them. I liked the sound of that. I was all for getting free games, especially if all I had to do was write my opinion of them afterward.

But I didn't have any writing experience then, and I couldn't see a magazine hiring me to write reviews—even in return for free games—just because I liked playing them. So rather than hit the phones and hear a series of rejections, I created my own games magazine.

The *Dallas Fort Worth Software Review* was never the most popular publication in the world. Some of the early editions might even have had a readership of . . . one. Two if a friend came over and happened to pick it up.

But when I called the software companies, told them I was a writer for the *Dallas Fort Worth Software Review,* and asked if they'd like to send me review copies of their new games, one question they never asked me was how big my readership was.

In fact, the only question they asked was, "What's your mailing address?"

When that first game was delivered to my door, and I laid the box on the kitchen table, I knew I'd had my first success. It wasn't money. I still hadn't made a dime. But I had a plan, the plan had worked, and I was off and running.

Soon games were pouring in from all the major software companies, and I didn't have time to play them all, let alone review them all. So I put an ad on an Internet bulletin board system—there were no forums back then—offering free games in return for reviews. That meant the games could continue to come in and I could continue to produce my little games magazine without breaking too much of a sweat. The small readership, however, was a problem.

That problem was solved by the Internet. When the Web really took off, I was ready. Playing with computers made me aware of its growth—and its potential—so I took all of the game-related content I had collected and put it on a new web site called WorldVillage.com. I also invited other writers to come in and submit content on any subject that interested them.

Today, WorldVillage is still going strong and continues to enjoy hundreds of thousands of visitors each month.

That's one Internet success story. As you'll see, it's not without its stumbling blocks—no business story ever is—but it has two key components that are essential for understanding (and duplicating) online success. They sum up the opportunity that the Web has brought to anyone with even a hint of entrepreneurial spirit.

The first is that online business success is open to *anyone*. I am a shining example of this. I'm not an expert. I still can't program. I still hire out the writing on many of my sites as well as their management to people who can do these things better than I can. I've always been interested in computers, but I'm not what you'd call a professional computer person.

The point is you don't need to complete a course in advanced programming. You don't have to know what HTML is, what a server looks like, or that Ruby on Rails isn't the name of a grunge band. Knowing those things might help—at least on the technical side. But you don't *need* to know them. I've met plenty of Internet millionaires who think that style sheets are programs handed out at fashion shows. It hasn't stopped them from creating successful site after successful site.

The second key component to the story of my first online success is that I still play computer games. They're fun. I might play them less now than I used to, but I still sit with my family sometimes in front of the screen as we battle monsters together. I am pleased to say that I am a Level 80 Warrior in World of Warcraft.

The reason the *Dallas Fort Worth Software Review* and then WorldVillage succeeded was that I was doing something I loved. I didn't set out to make money. I set out with the idea of doing something that I enjoyed. Because I enjoyed it, I was willing to put time and effort into doing it well. And because I put time and effort into doing it well, other people enjoyed it, too.

When that happens, there's always an opportunity to make money, especially on the Internet.

That's what this book is all about.

It's about what happens when you take a passion, place it on a platform that's open to anyone who wants to climb on to it, and then plug in the pipes that bring in the cash.

The result sounds a lot like KaChing.

So, Just How Easy Is It to Begin Building a Web Site?

To someone whose only experience on the Internet is reading the news, checking the sports scores, or perhaps answering e-mail, the online world can look pretty daunting.

Telling an Internet user that there's a fortune to be made online is a bit like telling a moviegoer that there are millions to be made in movies. Of course there are ... if you know how to handle a camera, write a script, find the production money, hire actors, edit the footage, and distribute the film. If you know how to do all that—and can make movies that people actually want to see—then, sure, you can make millions.

But creating successful web sites is not like shooting successful movies. Creating movie blockbusters is complicated. Creating Internet content is very, very simple. It was always meant to be simple, and today it's easier than it's ever been.

You can now be online with a new web site in less time than it takes to read this page.

And you can do it for free.

You won't hear your first KaChing right away. You'll still have to stock the site with content, plug in the systems that will pour in the cash, and let people know you're around. That will take a little time. But it won't require any skills more specialized than the ability to press a mouse button or choose an option in a drop-down menu.

It wasn't always like this. Although the Internet was always meant to be a place that anyone could use and anyone could build on, for a long time that really meant anyone who had the patience to read a programming manual the size of a shoebox.

Today, the Internet really has met its promise of being a truly democratic space. Those with a desire to earn and a willingness to learn as they go can have the beginnings of a profitable online business in minutes.

Usually, that takes one of two forms.

The traditional method has always been to create a web site from scratch. You bought a domain name from a service like GoDaddy.com, rented space on a hosting service, and placed the domain on the host's server. Then you used a special program to write the code and upload the pages. Whenever users entered the address of one of those pages in their Web browser, your page appeared on their screen.

This is still how most web sites work. It's how most of mine work. Doing it all manually provides the greatest amount of flexibility. But it's a little tricky, as it takes time to learn—or money to pay someone who already knows how to do it—and it's no longer necessary.

Web developers have made complete templates available to anyone who wants to use them. The prices vary. Some companies offer them for free; others charge thousands of dollars for a template that's unique, easy to customize, and filled with the latest Flash animation.

Whichever option you choose—and both types are no more than a quick search away—once you've bought your domain, all you have to do is upload the template and fill it with your content.

Alternatively, you can also use a content management system like Joomla! or Drupal. These are free programs that act as a kind of storage system for web site publishers. They sound frightening, but they've actually simplified web publishing enormously. Once you've taken the first leap of buying a domain and placing it on a server—a process that will take even the newest of publishers just a few nervous minutes—they'll allow you to add articles and use modules and extensions to place all sorts of preprogrammed goodies, such as RSS feeds, sidebars, and automated storefronts, on your web pages.

The first steps might feel a little strange. But once you have even a basic web site up and running, you won't be able to stop. You'll be experimenting and playing, and in no time at all you'll have become something of a web development expert simply because you're enjoying it. It happens. And it happens because it's now so simple.

Web site templates might have taken the sweat out of design, but there's an even easier and faster way to get on the Web. When Evan Williams, who would later go on to help create Twitter, launched Blogger in August 1999, he continued a process of simplification that cracked the Internet wide open.

A *blog* (short for "web log") is a very simple type of web site. Instead of having multiple static pages, the content on blogs is updated regularly and displayed in chronological order. That keeps readers coming back to see what's new. Older content gets buried but can be recovered from archives and by using searches based on keywords and subjects.

The benefit of blogs has always been their simplicity. While you can now upload all sorts of content, including video and real-time Twitter streams, writing a blog is not much different from writing in Microsoft Word, then saving it on the Internet so that everyone can see it. The attraction of a blog is always the content. If you can say something interesting—about any topic at all—you can build a successful blog.

Evan Williams certainly made a success of Blogger. Ten years later, Google bought the site for an undisclosed sum, and now Blogger is said to have 300 million active readers who consume the 388 million words uploaded through the service every single day (Figure 1.1).

Blogger, of course, now has plenty of competitors. Word-Press.org provides a lot more flexibility. It's open source, which means that anyone can build on it and create plug-ins that give publishers even more options. But unlike blogs on Blogger, it doesn't

Figure 1.1 Getting started with Blogger is really easy and takes only a minute.

come with hosting. Before you can use WordPress, you have to buy a domain name and place it on a host. You'll then need to download WordPress's blogging program from WordPress.org and upload it to your server. It's not difficult, but it takes just a little effort.

WordPress.com, on the other hand (as opposed to Word-Press.org), works exactly like Blogger. Your domain name will be [yourchosenname].WordPress.com. It's free, and you won't need to fiddle around with a hosting service. But you also won't be able to place AdSense, Chitika, Yahoo!, or text link ads on the site. As you'll see in this book, that still leaves plenty of other options, but WordPress.com wasn't really built for moneymaking, and the people behind it take a pretty dim view of revenue generation on these sites.

The best option is to use Blogger just to get your feet wet. I like to call it "blogging with training wheels." Then, once you have a handle on blogging, move up to WordPress.org or MovableType (www.movabletype.com).

There's a good chance, though, that you're already online, either with your own web site or a blog. You may have created them yourself from scratch, or you may have paid a developer to create your site(s) for you. Both options are fine.

I'm not going to talk you through the first steps of launching a blog or creating a web site. That information is available everywhere (including in my previous books), and it really is so simple now that the best way to learn how to do it is just to do it. Go to Blogger.com, register, and start writing. Don't be afraid to make mistakes, and don't be in too much of a hurry. Just enjoy the experience. That enjoyment will keep you moving forward.

At the beginning of this section, I pointed out that while you can start developing web sites and blogs in minutes, it will take you a little longer to start earning money with them. That's because you need *content* and *readers,* both of which take time to build.

Installing a system that can persuade people to give you money on the other hand is now quick and simple.

From Blogging to KaChing

Back in the old days, at the end of the twentieth century, there was a very easy and almost foolproof way to make a ton of money with a web site: You registered a domain, placed it on a server, and started writing.

You didn't write content. You wrote a business plan, and in that business plan you included the word *advertising* about three times in each sentence. Then you bought a plane ticket to California, met with a venture capitalist, showed off your business plan, and waited patiently while he or she wrote a check for several million dollars in return for 1 percent of your new company.

For some of those investors, that actually turned out to be a smart move. The start-up would go on to attract lots of users and would be bought by an even bigger company, making lots of money for the developer and the investor. The company that bought it, on the other hand, was often left with a big write-off.

The problem was that while everything looked good on paper, no one had come up with a reliable way to turn lots of users into piles of cash.

It was as though someone had invented the shopping mall before anyone had invented the cash register. Lots of people were coming into the stores, but with no way to spend their money, they were walking right back out with it.

Google changed all of that. It did this in two ways.

First, it created a search engine that made finding content both easy and accurate. Before Google launched in 1998, Internet users searching for Web content through sites like Yahoo! and Lycos needed to either browse categories or check results based on the number of times a keyword appeared on a page. That didn't always give them the best results. It meant that poor sites could game the system by stuffing pages with keywords, thereby sending the traffic and its benefits to the wrong people.

Sergey Brin's and Larry Page's idea of ranking sites according to the number of times other sites linked to them meant that their search engine didn't just deliver the right results, it also delivered the best results.

Suddenly, the Web wasn't just a random collection of sites that were difficult to navigate. It was a world that came with its own tour guide, who could point out the best places for anyone to visit regardless of their subject of interest.

If you wanted to know about stamp collecting, architecture, or celebrity news, Google would tell you. And it would not just tell you which site mentioned those things.

That was incredibly useful, and it enabled Google to quickly pick up vast numbers of Internet users keen to find a shortcut to the best content on the Web.

Up to that point, all Google had done was build a service users liked. No one was paying for it. Google still hadn't invented a cash register. That happened in 2000, when Google began accepting ads on its search results pages. Because the ads displayed depended on the search term the user entered, they were always relevant. And because they were text-based, they were also unobtrusive. Ads were displayed based on the price the advertiser was willing to pay, as well as the number of click-throughs they had received in the past.

It wasn't a completely new idea. (A site called Goto.com, which would eventually become Yahoo! Search Marketing, had been selling ads in a similar way. Yahoo! even sued Google for patent

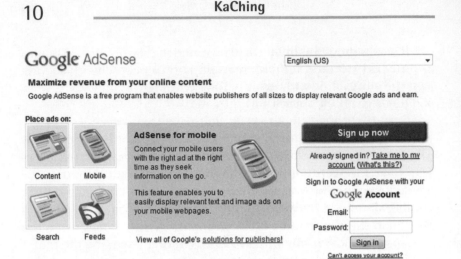

Figure 1.2   Google's AdSense program: The service that launched a million KaChings.

infringement in a case that was settled out of court.) But it did create the Internet's loudest KaChing ever. Even if the idea didn't come out of nowhere, Google certainly developed and implemented it better than anyone else. Today, Google is said to have 82.7 percent of the worldwide search market. In 2008, its total revenues, almost all from advertising, amounted to more than $21.8 billion.

That was good news for Google. The company had created a cash register that enabled it to accept money from companies that wanted to approach the millions of users it was picking up each day.

But the good news for everyone else was that Google also handed out cash registers free of charge to any Web publisher who wanted one.

The invention of AdWords, the system that Google uses to sell advertising space, might have made a deafening KaChing sound. But through AdSense (the publishing side of AdWords) that ring has been echoing around the Web ever since (Figure 1.2).

It's a system that's open to anyone with a web site. Sign up at www.google.com/adsense and you'll be given a few lines of code that you can place on your Web pages. That code will automatically serve up ads from Google's inventory, and those ads will be based on the content of your web site.

It's an incredible thing.

You get relevant, unobtrusive ads, and you are paid every time one of your users clicks one.

It has to be the easiest KaChing in the history of commerce.

Sure, there are strategies you can use to maximize your earnings. When I first started using AdSense back in 2004, I made $40 a month. That's not KaChing. That's ker-splat.

But once I'd optimized my ads, blended them into my sites, and tested a bunch of different strategies, my AdSense income skyrocketed. Today, I regularly receive monthly checks from Google for more than $15,000.

Now *that's* KaChing!

What's important here, though, isn't just the amounts. It's the simplicity.

Web site templates, content management systems, and blogging platforms have opened up Internet publishing to anyone who knows how to turn on a computer and operate a keyboard. With Google AdSense, we now have a way of turning those sites into money that's just as simple.

We have the store, and we have the cash register.

In fact, we now have lots of cash registers. We have different types of cash registers on our sites, and we can put them in different places. Google's AdSense system is primarily a cost-per-click (CPC) program. As a publisher, you are paid every time someone clicks on an ad. But you can also use other services to be paid on a cost-per-action (CPA) basis: When someone buys, you earn a commission. You can also earn on a cost-per-mille (CPM) basis: You receive a small amount of money for every thousand times your Web page is loaded and the ad shown, regardless of what the people who see it do.

And that's just advertising. As you'll see throughout this book, there are now plenty of other ways of generating a KaChing from a successful web site, including information products, coaching, and membership sites.

This is the New Web Order. It's a place that's open to anyone who wants to join. The pioneering days are over. The strategies, methods, and approaches have all been tested, proven, and simplified. The tools are available, they're free, and they're waiting for anyone who's willing to pick them up, use them, and learn how they work.

Perhaps the best way to think of Web publishing today is to compare it to photography. Anyone can take a simple picture. A basic digital camera costs next to nothing and will let you shoot pictures of your family, your cat, and the sunset at the beach. When you take good pictures, you'll get a little thrill of satisfaction that will encourage you to take more. It won't be long before you're thinking of upgrading and buying a fancy camera that will let you play with exposure and focusing and do all of the other things that fancy cameras do.

That will encourage you to learn about photography, and the more you learn and the more you shoot, the better you'll get. You might never be commissioned to shoot the cover of *Vanity Fair,* but as long as you enjoy what you're doing, your skills will improve to a level that allows you to perhaps sell the odd photo on eBay or iStockphoto, or hire yourself out for weddings and events.

On the Internet, anyone can get started with a simple web site or blog. You can plug in AdSense or one of the other Internet cash registers that are now easily available. You can begin making money—and you can continue making even more money as you grow and learn.

It's not a process that takes place overnight. In fact, the learning process never ends. But the sooner you start, the sooner you'll hear that first KaChing.

To get started though, you'll need a topic. Just as store owners have to know what kind of products they want to sell, so publishers have to know what kind of content they want to offer.

It's a vital question, and it's something I discuss in Chapter 2.

Your Uniqueness Equals Cash

We've seen that the Internet has democratized opportunities in two ways. The low cost and ease of building a web site now means that anyone can own online real estate. You don't need to know anything about the Internet to put up a blog or create a site. You can buy them almost ready-made, off the shelf. What flat-pack design has done for amateur furniture makers, templates, content management systems, and blogging software have done for web sites.

And you don't have to waste brain cells trying to think up ways to monetize your site, either. With Google handing out cash registers, there's always one very simple way of making money from your users. Once you are used to that method, it's just a short step to all of the other strategies discussed in this book.

There is another way that the Web has opened up to everyone, though, and it's no less important.

It's made us all into experts.

Or rather, it's enabled all of us to earn from our expertise, which isn't quite the same thing, because you've always been an expert. You might not have a doctorate in cheesecake making or a Nobel Prize for your contributions to world crocheting, but if you know more about those things than most people do, then you're an expert on that topic.

Note that I don't say that you have to know more about those topics than *everyone* else does. You don't have to be the world's leading expert to earn from your knowledge on the Internet. You just need to have knowledge that other people don't have but want.

Everybody has knowledge like that.

If you do origami in your spare time, then you're an expert on origami. Sure, there are people who can fold paper better than you can. But they don't have a web site that shares their knowledge. You do. (If they do have a web site, then their site discusses ways of making paper animals, while yours will explain how to fold paper boxes.)

If you like sports, then maybe you're an expert on your local football team. If you're into cooking, then perhaps you're an expert on barbecuing, baking cookies, or making whatever type of food you like to cook the most.

Everybody is an expert in something because everyone has to fill 24 hours of his or her day with something. Even if you spend half that time on the sofa watching television and the other half in bed sleeping, then you're an expert on sofas, daytime soaps, and a dozen ways to waste your time. As long as people want to know about those things, the Internet will give you an opportunity to make money from that knowledge.

You might not pick up millions of users. It's certainly possible that if you launch a web site about knitting with yellow wool, you'll find that only a fraction of the total number of people interested in knitting will stop by to look. But those people will likely be dedicated knitters. They'll be the ones most likely to click on an ad, buy an affiliate product, or sign up for a paid subscription to your newsletter. It might be a tiny subject, but because it's on the Web and therefore available to everyone, everywhere, you can land enough users to bring in enough money to start building a profitable online business.

That's the value of the long tail—the Internet's ability to build revenue-generating audiences for the most specialized of topics. And it means that any knowledge you have has value and can generate a KaChing online.

Choosing Your Niche

The first step is the easiest—and the most enjoyable. In fact, the best way to know you're doing it right is if you enjoy it.

Yet even at this stage, people still get it wrong.

I've lost count of the number of people who have approached me at conferences and workshops and asked me what their web site should be about. I can't help them there. I have no idea what *your* web site should be about either. I do know the principle that should underlie the subject of every profitable web site: It must be a topic its publisher enjoys and is interested in.

Forget about the apparent value of the topic for now. Forget about the fact that some topics are more likely to make money than others. Build a web site that's designed only to make money and you might hear a little KaChing in the beginning, but by the time you've built up a large enough knowledge of Internet business to make big money, you'll have run out of ideas and be so bored with the subject that you'll stop adding good content. Maintaining the site will feel like a chore, and when that happens, you might as well have a j-o-b. It will feel just as painful.

It won't be as profitable though, because when you get bored with your site, you can be certain that it won't be long before your users get bored with your site, too. The Internet is filled with the skeletons of dead web sites that started with the idea of making cash and then faded away as the publisher became bored and moved on.

When you're looking for your niche, don't think about money. Don't worry about the KaChing. That will come. Think instead about what interests you.

What do you spend the bulk of your day doing? What do you do in your spare time? What books do you read when you have a free moment? All of those things can be topics for a profitable web site, whether you spend your day climbing mountains or battling aliens on your Xbox.

In practice, you can divide your choices into two categories: your professional life and your personal life.

Your professional life is always going to yield rich pickings. People already pay you for that expertise. If you're a plumber, people call you because you know how to fix a dripping tap and they don't.

If you're an administrator, you know how to keep an office in order and deal with paperwork. Those are valuable skills. And if you're a doctor, a lawyer, an accountant, or anything else, you don't need me to tell you how valuable the information in your head is.

Whatever your job, your experience and training have given you information you can use to earn a living. The Internet has given you a place where you can share that knowledge. And all of the revenue systems that have developed online mean that you can turn that knowledge into KaChing.

One of my favorite sites, for example, is Tim Carter's AsktheBuilder.com (Figure 2.1). Tim is a former contractor and home builder who has been online for a long time. He first set up his site in 1993, and it's seen a lot of incarnations since then. One thing that hasn't changed is the quality and the subject of his content. His articles are syndicated in newspapers nationwide, and he even ended a radio career so that he could focus on something that could make even more money: his web site.

Figure 2.1 Tim Carter's AsktheBuilder.com is a great example of someone making money online with his professional knowledge. Note the banner ad, Google search box, e-books, newsletter, and shop. Those are just some of the ways Tim generates KaChing online.

Tim posts content that explains how to put up shelves, grout tiles, refinish stair treads, and a whole lot more. Some of that information appears in articles, and some is posted in short videos that can also be seen on YouTube.

That's valuable information. If you wanted to learn how to do these things, you'd probably have to pay for an expensive college course. If you wanted to hire someone to do these things for you, it would cost you hundreds or even thousands of dollars. It's knowledge that's taken Tim years of training and experience to build up.

Tim gives it away for free, and he uses the Internet's revenue systems to make money from it.

Carolyn E. Wright does something similar at PhotoAttorney.com. Carolyn is an amateur photographer and a professional lawyer who specializes in the law as it relates to photographers. Her web site, which takes the form of a blog, provides articles about the law and photography (Figure 2.2).

Again, it's valuable information. When Carolyn explains the relevance of a recent court case involving a photographer, people who take pictures, especially professional photographers, realize

Figure 2.2 Carolyn E. Wright's blog, PhotoAttorney.com, lets one lawyer earn money from her professional knowledge.

that they're getting gold dust. Lawyers charge a fortune for advice. Carolyn is giving away her professional opinion for nothing.

What does she get in return?

She certainly gets branding. When a photographer finds that a company is using one of his or her pictures without permission or is being sued by an unhappy client, Carolyn's firm is the first place that person will turn for legal representation. But Carolyn isn't relying on that. Her site also announces her speaking engagements, her workshops, her books (both legal and photographic), her legal packages (including trademark registration, debt collection, and consulting), and even affiliate links supplied by Amazon.

The web site alone is unlikely to be a replacement for Carolyn's professional services. But it does allow her to create an additional revenue stream from her professional skills.

It's certainly possible to make money online with a web site that draws on your professional knowledge.

But you can also do the same thing with the knowledge that you pick up doing what you love. Carolyn E. Wright does this as well. She has chosen a niche within the law that interests her as a photographer. That means she derives even more pleasure from her job than she might if she had chosen to specialize in real estate law, for example, or patent law. Because she's chosen to work in a niche that interests her personally, her blog is interesting to read and people are more likely to come and read it.

Not everyone is as lucky as Carolyn E. Wright. Many people have a job they enjoy (if they're fortunate), then do something completely different on the weekend because they enjoy doing that even more. The good news is that you can earn money online from that information, too.

In fact, this is where the Web really rolls out its golden opportunity.

Offline, it's very difficult to make money from a hobby. Lots of people dream about becoming professional writers, designing computer games, or taking photos for a living. For the most interesting and exciting jobs, the competition is always fierce, and the number of people who want them tend to push the pay down to bargain levels.

With the Web, anyone can now make money from a hobby.

Perhaps the most famous person to do this is Darren Rowse. When Darren started his first blog at TheLivingRoom.org back in 2002, he intended it to be a personal diary that would discuss his views on life in his native Australia, politics, and the church. He didn't expect the site to make money, but it did become popular with members of the emergent church movement in Australia. Again, he was writing about something that was important to him, so he picked up an audience who found the topic important to them, too.

The following year, Darren started a second blog, this time about digital cameras. He planned to use the site to show off some of his own images, but he also found that whenever he posted a review of a camera, his views went up by a factor of 20. Encouraged, he posted more camera reviews—and received even more traffic.

Things really took off though when Darren added AdSense ads to the blog in October 2003—although they initially took off very slowly. In his first month, even on a site with thousands of readers every day, Darren made just $1.40 per day, enough to cover his server costs but not much more. But he kept going, and he kept watching his ad revenues increase. By December, he was making $6 per day, in January $9, and in February $10. The following month his ad revenues jumped by 50 percent. Today, Digital Photography School (www.digital-photography-school.com) and Darren's second site, ProBlogger (www.problogger.com), generate up to 100,000 page views a day and earn more than $20,000 for Darren in ad revenue each month.

And those are just two of the many blogs that Darren now runs.

Those two sites are great examples of the two different kinds of profitable sites that anyone can build. Darren isn't a professional photographer. He's not even an expert photographer. There are plenty of people on the Web with much deeper photographic knowledge and much better pictures. Today, Darren writes very little of the content that appears on Digital Photography School, offering space instead to photographers who contribute their own articles in return for the kind of visibility that only a successful blog can deliver.

But it's a subject that Darren is passionate about, one he knows a lot about, and one he enjoys publishing about. That passion comes across clearly in the quality of the content on the site, and it's that devotion that brings in other equally dedicated readers.

Darren is now a professional blogger. In addition to running Digital Photography School, he is also a cofounder of b5media, a stable of around 300 blogs on a range of different subjects. That's given him a huge amount of valuable knowledge about what it takes to create a successful web site. He makes that information available on www.ProBlogger.com and again earns money from ads and affiliate links on those pages.

Whereas Digital Photography School is a blog about Darren's passion, ProBlogger is a blog about his profession. Both earn money.

The Value of Your Niche—How Keywording Can Boost the Price of Your Passion

While web sites about either your profession or your passion can earn money, they won't necessarily make the same amount of money. The most important factors that determine the value of a web site are:

- ◆ Content
- ◆ Traffic
- ◆ Revenue systems

Content includes quality and quantity (the more frequently you post, the more views you'll win), but it also covers topic. Some topics simply pay more than others. You might be able to get a KaChing by publishing a web site on any subject at all, but the sound alone won't tell you how much money is going into the cash register until you count it.

That was something that Darren Rowse discovered very quickly. His first blog, which was mostly about spirituality, built an audience. But because it's a topic with little commercial value, it didn't generate much money.

A site about the Bible, for example, will largely attract ads offering Bible study courses. These might be supplied by nonprofit or religious organizations that have few funds to pay for ad clicks and little to gain when they do pick up a lead. The amount the publisher will pay for a click will be relatively low.

However, when Darren began writing camera reviews, he didn't just pick up lots of additional readers, he also picked up higher-paying ads. Someone reading camera reviews is exactly the sort of person that camera stores most want to attract. Those stores will happily compete to put their name—and a link to their online store—in front of those readers. The result will be much higher payments each time a reader clicks an on ad, because there's a reasonable chance that a percentage of those readers will pay an advertiser hundreds of dollars for a new camera.

This is where things can start to become a little dangerous. There's no shortage of companies on the Web offering lists of the highest-paying AdSense keywords. They certainly look useful. At a glance, you'll be able to see that a web site about "purchase structured settlements," for example, can generate $53.48 for every click on an AdSense ad. A page about a "Phoenix DUI attorney" can bring up ads worth $50, and "California mesothelioma doctors" are worth $46.14 per click.

Compared to the usual dollar or two per click, those look like giant KaChings. Generate just three or four clicks on ads like that every day and you could be making a cool $6,000 a month in additional income.

If only it were that easy. It might work, at least for a while. You could create a web site that focused on structured settlements— whatever they are—and put in the AdSense code. If you're also prepared to put in the effort to be able to write about the topic intelligently for a while (because traffic takes time to build), then you might well find yourself generating some income.

But it's not a fun way to work, and when you're not writing about a topic you enjoy, it will feel like work, and it will be hard to do well enough to earn money consistently. That doesn't mean you shouldn't try writing about a subject purely for the high-paying keywords. But I wouldn't recommend it. I think that choosing a topic you enjoy will always be better in the long run. You might be packing away fewer dollars for each KaChing but you'll generating more KaChings, and most important, you'll be having fun while you're doing it—so you'll be able to keep doing it.

But there are things you can do to ensure the subjects you blog about within those topics are the highest-paying subjects possible.

That's important. Writing about photography in general might deliver ads from stock agencies or camera shops. Writing about equine photography on the other hand might deliver ads from stables and horse breeders—and those ads might pay much more!

When you're searching for subjects about which to publish, knowing that the ads for one subject are worth more than the ads for another can help to guide you toward the best revenues.

Google, though, won't tell you how much you're receiving for each click on a specific ad. Nor is Google the only company that should be serving ads on your web site. However you're receiving your ads, you should always be tracking the clicks and the money those clicks generate.

You have to do this yourself. Keyword value lists will give you only a vague idea of what a term or a subject is worth. In practice, the amounts change constantly, and they can be different on different web sites. Google uses a practice called Smart Pricing that takes into account not just the amount the advertiser has bid to appear on Web pages, but the actions that users take when they reach the advertiser's site. The higher the value of your users to the advertiser, the more advertisers will have to pay. And the reverse is also true: A site with visitors who have little connection to the subject will receive little for each ad click, even when the advertiser has expressed a willingness to pay more.

Once you've decided on an overall topic for your web site, you should then write on different subtopics and track the revenues that those pages generate. Just as Darren Rowse noticed that camera reviews generated the most views and the highest revenues, so you should soon be able to see which subjects interest your readers and which bring up the highest-earning ads.

Niches Are Nice, but Micro-Niches Create Nicer KaChings

Let's say that you're excited about gardening. Every weekend you take a trip to the garden center, load up on plants, and spend your spare time digging around trees, laying down irrigation pipes, pruning branches, pulling up weeds, creating mulch, and doing all of the other things that green-thumb types do to keep their gardens looking pretty.

That's not me, but let's say it's you.

You sign up at Blogger.com and write a few articles about gardening. You also join Google's AdSense program, receive your AdSense code, and place it on your pages, optimizing the units so that they blend into the page. You leave comments on a few other gardening blogs and join forum discussions to let people know you're there.

There's a good chance that before the week is out, you'll have received your first KaChing. One morning, you'll look at your AdSense stats and find that instead of the total earnings column saying 0.00, it now says 0.10.

KaChing!

Okay, that's not a very loud KaChing. You might think that dime isn't going to change your life, but if you let it, it will. Forget the amount. Think of the principle. You've written about a topic you love and picked up money by doing it online. It's small money now, but if you continue, those amounts are going to grow, and that KaChing is going to get louder.

So you continue writing articles. You pay attention to search engine optimization, and you use link exchanges to build up traffic. As your traffic increases, so does your income.

You also keep track of the performance of your articles. AdSense provides Channels, which are tracking tools that allow you to follow the performance of individual ad units. So you create separate channels for articles about fruit trees, flowers, lawn care, and bonsai management, and when you compare those channels, what you find is that articles about bonsai trees do particularly well. Traffic spikes every time you write about bonsai trees; your click-through rate (the percentage of users who click on an ad) is 3.5 percent instead of your usual 2.5 percent, and the average price per click on these ads is a dollar instead of the 60 cents you tend to pick up on other topics.

Fantastic. Now you have a blog about gardening that's making money, and you know of a specific gardening topic that's particularly valuable. That's a real KaChing.

You could continue as usual, making sure that you include plenty of regular posts about bonsai trees. But you could also be a little clever. You know that bonsai might be a small part of gardening, but it's still a broad enough topic to stand on its own. So you create a second free blog on Blogger dedicated to bonsai trees. You talk about it on the first blog to help build up the audience and keep posting content, keep including the AdSense code, and keep tracking the results.

Because this site is about *only* bonsai, you can be sure that everyone who reads it has a strong interest in that topic. More of them then will click the ads that are now from bonsai growers and suppliers of bonsai pots and training wires. The keywords will be more relevant and more concentrated, and as the site grows, it will appear higher in search engine results. And because it's focused, other sites on the topic will talk about it, giving you even more traffic and even higher earnings.

That's usually the way the Web works. The more specific the topic of a web site, the more dedicated the audience, the easier it is to market, and the more the site's users are worth to companies active in that niche.

Your first choice then will be to decide whether you want to create a niche site based on knowledge from your profession or knowledge from your passion.

The second choice, which you'll make once you've been online for a while, is which micro-niche you'll write about next. Sure, you'll then have to write two blogs, but because those two topics interest you anyway, writing about them should be fun—and the revenues will make it all worthwhile.

Best of all, because you have one site that's already successful, you should find that the second one is able to get off to a flying start. When Darren Rowse started Twitip.com, a blog about Twitter, he had 1,000 RSS subscribers within a week of launch. Those people were signing up because they already knew his ProBlogger site and trusted Darren to deliver interesting information on his new blog as well.

As you expand the topics of your Internet business, you should find that easy growth happens for you, too.

You're Not That Unique—Building Your Community

The goal of this chapter is to show how the things that interest you have value. Whether you work as a builder or a lawyer, you have professional knowledge that can bring you money online. Whether you're interested in gardening or photography, you have passions that can bring you money online.

Everyone has a unique set of interests, a unique degree of interest in those topics, a unique collection of information about them, and a unique way of describing them.

But the interests themselves aren't unique. If you're the only person in the world interested in the sewing patterns on the sails of ancient Greek triremes, then you're going to struggle to make money online. You won't have any users, and the AdSense code will look at your content, shrug, and serve up something vaguely related.

But because other people are interested in the subject of your web site, you have an audience. Your advertisers have a market. And you have a community.

A community is more than just a collection of people. It's a group with a shared interest and a shared goal. That interest could be gardening, jewelry making, American ghost towns, or anything else. The goal could be a better garden, jewelry that people want to buy, or the discovery of more ghost towns. The interest and the goal themselves aren't what's important. What is important is that the community feels tightly knit and that each member feels that he belongs. That closeness helps to keep your site going in the long term and makes it less likely that users break away to competitors. It's why businesses offer membership plans and loyalty programs that reward customers and keep them close.

You'll want to do whatever you can to keep that community together. That group of people with an interest in bonsai trees, photography, home repairs, or whatever your site is about should see you as one of its leaders. It should regard your site as a prime source for information about its topic.

When that happens, you draw lots of easy traffic to your web site. You are talked about constantly. The price of advertising on your site shoots through the roof, and you find it very easy to grow and sell.

In the past, turning your readers into a community used to be fairly difficult. You could look at your site statistics and see all sorts of information about your users. You could see where they were located, what search term they entered into a search engine before they reached you, which site they reached you from, and even which kind of browser they used to view your site.

But you didn't really get to see them. Users were numbers in a table, faceless figures who determined your month's online revenues. That's all changed.

Now, users are people. You can see their names in their comments. You can read about their lives on Twitter, you can become friends on Facebook, and you can form professional relationships on LinkedIn.

Those are all important elements in a successful site. Users have such a huge choice of Web pages to read and sites to visit that you have to keep them entertained, interested, and engaged if you're going to ensure that your site grows. You want your visitors to see you not as another source to check every now and then, but as a friend they have online. Reading your web site should be as much a part of their daily routine as checking e-mail and visiting their Facebook page.

First, encourage people to leave comments on your blog. You should find that readers do that anyway, and it's a fantastic thing. Seeing the results of a KaChing in your stats table is always encouraging, but when you get unsolicited comments from readers saying, "Great post!" and "Fascinating article," you really do feel you're on the right track.

Those sorts of comments are nice ego boosters, but you want more than that. You want users to leave their opinions and continue the discussion you've started. If you've written a post explaining how to create good compost, you want other gardeners to chime in with their composting tips. If your post is an opinion piece about the noise electric hedge trimmers make, then you want other people to join the argument, whether they agree with you or not.

Most of all, you want comments on your blog submitted by professionals. That shows that your blog has influence, is respected, and has content that can't be found anywhere else—even if you didn't write that content yourself.

There are things you can do to encourage comments. Writing about controversial subjects is perhaps the easiest. Every niche has issues about which people feel strongly. Editors on news sites know that when they write a news story about abortion, Israel, or health care, they're going to get page after page of comments. If they write about the cost of potato chips in Sweden, however, it's unlikely that they'll get any.

You shouldn't be writing about controversial topics all the time. That would make your site look predictable. But you should know which subjects are most likely to cause a storm in your community.

You should know too the effect that storm is going to have on you. My blog, JoelComm.com, is mostly about entrepreneurship and online marketing. Occasionally though, I'll let fly on a subject that I feel strongly about it. It could be politics, business, or people not washing their hands after going to the bathroom. Those posts always generate lots of extra comments, but they can also irritate people—especially people with dirty hands (and they know who they are). Writing about controversial topics might cost you a few users who strongly disagree with you, but overall it's a winner. Those who remain feel a closer connection with you. You're not just a web site, you're a person with opinions, thoughts, and feelings. You're someone just like your readers: a friend and a member of their community.

Comments are one way for your readers to communicate with you and to share their thoughts with other members of your community. It's social media, though, that's really made the difference for publishers trying to turn their users into a community.

The three most important sites for an Internet publisher are Facebook, Twitter, and LinkedIn. Each site has its strengths and each serves a different purpose.

You're probably already using Facebook to keep in touch with old friends and colleagues. Once you launch a web site, it's worth creating a Facebook fan page for your site, which acts just like your regular Facebook page. You'll be able to use status updates to tell people when you've published a new post. You'll also be able to create discussions on topics that are important to your community. Most of all, you'll be able to see who is reading your posts, and they'll be able to see you. That helps to create a much more powerful connection between you and your readers and between your readers themselves.

LinkedIn is similar, but it has a greater emphasis on business relationships. You should certainly create a profile for your site and your business on LinkedIn if you're going to be publishing anything related to commerce, but even sites dedicated to passions rather than professions should be using LinkedIn. It's another useful link between you and your community.

I use both of those sites, but these days I use Twitter even more. In fact, I even use a special application on Facebook that lets me send my Twitter updates to Facebook so that they appear as status updates (Figure 2.3).

Figure 2.3 Twitter helps me to build my personal brand and talk directly to my community, but look at what else I've crammed into my Twitter page: sponsored tweets, announcements, personal updates, links to blog posts, URLs, and plugs for my products.

For a publisher, Twitter can be like lifting the curtain and taking your readers backstage. While a blog post is carefully crafted and researched, a Twitter update can be spur of the moment. It can be something as important as an announcement of a new product release or as simple as a description of what you're having for lunch. Each of those posts helps bring you a little closer to your audience.

Because your followers on Twitter can also write to you directly and publicly—and receive a reply—that relationship becomes personal. I don't think there's a more powerful community-building tool than Twitter—and its benefits don't stop there.

You can also use one of Twitter's widgets to post on your blog tweets that you've written, tweets that have been written about you, and even tweets that have been written about your topic. That's valuable and dynamic free content. You can set up your RSS feed so that it feeds into Twitter, letting people on the site know automatically when you've posted new content. And you can include affiliate links and ads that let you earn money directly from tweeting.

It's a hugely valuable tool that can act as a strong glue holding your community together.

Once you've built that community, you should find that you've given your site the kind of foundation that will keep it secure in the long term.

The Seven Keys to Success

In this chapter, I've tried to demonstrate two of the most important conditions of online success. In fact, they're the two most important conditions of success at whatever you do:

1. Do what you do best.

2. Do what you love.

When you're doing both of those things, I think it takes a special effort *not* to succeed. The pleasure and satisfaction that comes from doing what you enjoy will keep you going even when the success you really want still seems far away.

When you're working in a field about which you know more than most, you'll have the assets that deliver the returns.

That's all very simple, and it makes choosing a topic for an online business—and then a more valuable subtopic—a very easy decision. It also makes building a community around your site very smooth. You're going to be interacting with people just like you, people with the same interests, concerns, and goals. That's like working every day with the sort of people you'd choose as friends. How many workplaces does that describe?

Those two principles are the foundation of success, but there's a little more to it than that. As I built up my business from a single site with computer game reviews into a multi-million-dollar company, and after speaking with dozens of other successful Internet entrepreneurs, I've come to recognize seven keys to success. They develop from the same starting point. You still have to focus on what makes you unique and what makes you happy, but once you've done that, you then have to do the following.

1. YOU HAVE TO DREAM

All the entrepreneurs I've met had a dream. Actually, they had lots of dreams. In some of those dreams, they were lying on the beach in Cancun with the surf lapping gently against their toes and threatening to wash away their piña colada.

But that's not the dream that moved them to set up their own business. A dream of material wealth, comfort, or a certain lifestyle is fine. It might be something to aim for in the distance. But it's a destination. It's not the engine that keeps you driving forward.

That's the dream of doing what you're passionate about.

Even lying on the beach can get old. It might take a little while, but you will eventually start to think of another trip to the sea the same way you think now about going back to the office after a weekend off. It's why retirees with condos in Miami still keep a hand in their old business and sometimes do a little freelance consulting on the side. If you enjoy your work, why stop?

That's the dream. If you were living *that* dream, each morning you'd leap out of bed ready to seize the day. Most people, of course, don't leap out of bed each morning. Most people aren't doing what they were born to do. If you're not following your passion—if you're not building your dream—then sadly, you are one of those people, at least for now.

Identifying your dream and following it aren't always easy, but it really shouldn't be that difficult. Most people have more than one dream and more than one passion. After I had turned my love of computer games into a successful web site, I turned my attention to something else that gave me pleasure, and still does . . . shopping!

Yes, I admit it. I don't just get a thrill from hearing a KaChing telling me I have money coming in. I also get a thrill from hearing the KaChing that tells me I'm *spending* money—especially when I'm buying something on sale. So after creating WorldVillage.com, I launched DealofDay.com, a site that helps people find bargains. The site gets over 25,000 visits a day and continues to grow.

Since then things have gotten better and better, and I don't think it's a coincidence. I believe that when you're doing what you were born to do, the path unfolds right in front of you. It might not be straight, and it certainly won't be bump-free. But it's yours; it takes you where you want to go, and it feels right.

Nor will it be the only path you take. Passions change over time. I started with a passion for computer games, and I still enjoy playing. But my mission is a lot bigger now. We grow and mature and change.

Today, whether you're taking your first steps and have yet to hear that first KaChing, or whether you have been online for a while and just want to know how to take in even more money, ask yourself whether you're doing what you love. Launch a site about your biggest passion and just see how much you enjoy building it.

Don't worry about the money. Do it for fun. I think it's inevitable that when you do enjoyable work in an environment that's as fertile and rich as the Internet, the rewards grow on their own.

2. YOU HAVE TO BELIEVE

Once you've identified your dream, you have to believe it's the right one.

You have to believe that your life has a plan and a purpose. That belief can take a number of different forms. Personally, I believe there is a God and that He has a plan for my life. Regardless, you have to believe that what you're doing is right—and right for you. With a belief and a dream, things start to happen.

But they don't always happen in quite the way you want. Businesses have ups and downs, and there will be times when your belief is tested. That certainly happened to me when I was starting out.

When I began building a web site, I had an investor. He provided $25,000, allowing me to quit my job and prepare to make my first million. By the summer, I had $1.37 left.

Things really weren't looking good and I had every reason to think that I should be doing something else. But I was certain that this was what I was supposed to do. I knew it.

I believed it.

Within a week I received an e-mail from a man in Seattle. I'd never heard of him, and I'd certainly never heard of the Japanese multimedia corporation he said he was representing. His e-mail said that the company wanted to license some of my web site content and localize it for the Japanese market.

I figured that would be worth a couple hundred bucks a month. Before I could say anything, he offered me $5,000 a month. We upsold him to $7,500 a month, and out of nowhere the company was saved.

You could say that was just dumb luck. But I don't think so. If I hadn't believed that I was doing the right thing, I would have given up long before that e-mail came in. When you believe that you're doing what you're supposed to be doing, things happen. You stick to it and you work hard, even when the quitters would have long since given up.

If you want to be successful, you have to believe that there is a plan and a purpose in your life. Forget about what your friends say. Don't listen to your relatives if they try to change your mind. You have to believe the truth: that you have a path. Once you've found it, you have to keep doing it.

3. YOU HAVE TO PREPARE

Dreams and beliefs are mental things. But to achieve success you have to break a sweat, too. You have to prepare.

Before I became a mobile DJ, I researched equipment. Before I give a talk, I prepare the slides. And before I create a new product, I examine what people want from it and what I need to do to find the up-to-date, practical information they need.

I prepare.

Whatever the subject matter of your web site, you have to commit yourself to having the latest knowledge on your topic. You have to understand how the field ranges, who the important influences are, and which topics are most in demand.

It's a process that takes time—and that's why it's so valuable. The information that you'll be offering through your site allows the people who read it to skip past some of that learning stage. Whether you're a professional plumber or an amateur photographer, your expertise is the result of years of practice and experience. That's an asset, and the next stage of the preparation is to understand which parts of that asset are the most valuable and how people most want to receive them.

Preparation means investing in yourself and in your success. It's a fundamental part of that success.

4. You Have to Act

Preparation is essential, but it brings a danger. I've come across plenty of people who buy the books, do the conferences, talk the talk . . . and yet never accomplish anything. They suffer the "paralysis of analysis."

You can never feel prepared enough. There's always more to learn, more to read, more to test. Preparation is all about answering questions: How much are the keywords in that subtopic worth? What happens if I put a different ad unit here? How many people really bought that e-book? How much did they pay for it, and how would my own differ? Every answer brings up three more questions.

Eventually, there comes a time when you just have to act, ready or not.

Back in 2006, I teamed up with my friend Eric Holmlund to create an online reality television show. We wanted it to be something like *The Apprentice,* but focused on Internet marketing. In each episode, a group of rising entrepreneurs would be set a task related to one aspect of building an online business, and the worst-performing candidate would be eliminated. The idea was simple enough, but the implementation? That was another story.

Eric had dabbled a little in film production—although nothing on this scale—and it was all completely new to me. We had no idea what we were letting ourselves in for. We spent months doing the research. We had to know what the program should include, what sort of people we'd want on it, what sorts of tasks we wanted to give the contestants, how to distribute and market the finished program, and of course, how to raise the funds and bring in revenue. It was a massive undertaking that took a huge amount of time and effort.

At some point though, we just had to dive in and see if we'd sink or swim. We swam.

I wish I could tell you it always works out that way. But it doesn't. Not every action will bring success. Entrepreneurs take risks. You have to be willing to put yourself out there, and you have to learn to fail fast.

Failure to take action is usually a result of FEAR: False Evidence Appearing Real. It's what happens when you believe a lie, when you're afraid of what might happen. You overcome fear when you take action.

5. You Have to Relate

There's a reason that I mentioned the value of community building so early in this book. It's vital to your success, and it's very easy to forget.

Being an entrepreneur, especially an Internet entrepreneur, looks like a lonely business. When you're starting out, it will be you, your computer . . . and that's all. Maybe you'll send e-mails to contractors—copywriters, designers, and programmers. Maybe you'll make the odd phone call to explain in more detail what you need, but you won't have the kind of face-to-face meetings that cement relationships in brick-and-mortar businesses.

That will be fine . . . for a while. But if you want to succeed—*really* succeed—it can't stay that way. The Internet, like every industry, is still about relationships. I found that out myself in the best way possible.

By 2005, I had written the first version of my AdSense e-book, a guide to all of the strategies that had worked for me in using Google's advertising program. The e-book sold a *lot* more than I expected, and I was looking for the next level. Both my wife and my friend Jeff Walker suggested going to Armand Morin's Big Seminar in Los Angeles. That didn't sound like a good idea to me. It's true that I had given AdSense a second look only after seeing someone's results at a workshop, but I'm really not one for sitting in a lecture hall and taking notes. In fact, I'm not really one for sitting at all.

But I listened to their advice and showed up. I discovered that I was already a celebrity of sorts. People knew about my book, and because my picture was on the web site, they knew who I was, too. I was part of a community and I didn't even know it!

The people I met at that conference have helped me ever since. They've told me about strategies that would have taken me years to discover and learn. They've introduced me to their audiences, as I've introduced them to mine. They've inspired me, taught me, and enhanced my understanding of every aspect of online business building. The relationships that I've built with the people I've met at conferences and workshops might well be my most valuable asset of all.

Forget about competition. There's enough to go around for everyone. Make contacts. Build friendships. Provide value without expecting any payback. In time, you should find that those investments in human relationships pay you back in spades.

6. You Have to Use Models

When you're looking to enjoy success, you want to enjoy it right now. You can't do that. Unless you win the lottery, wealth—and the freedom that wealth and success bring—come only as a result of investment of time and effort. Still, there are things you can do to reduce the amount of effort and time you need to invest.

One of the most important—and a vital aspect of your preparation—is looking at what other people have done.

There's very little that's completely new in the world. Growth tends to happen incrementally rather than in giant leaps. When someone else has achieved success, there's nothing wrong with looking at how they did it...and copying them, adding your own unique touches.

Once I'd achieved success with AdSense, I was happy to share what I'd learned so that others could do the same thing. It's a pattern I've followed myself, so it's only fair to give back.

Even when I sat down to create that book, I was following a model. It's the model that we use now in helping others publish their first book via my friends at Morgan James Publishing. The credibility that individuals garner by having their book published helps them to become the leading specialists in their fields, to create their web sites, and to benefit from exposure.

If it works, do it. And if someone else is achieving success, copy them.

Mentors are hugely valuable in providing models for your own success. They provide knowledge, they provide connections, and they provide relationships.

They also provide another key to your success.

7. You Have to Grow

One of my first mentors was a professional business coach. Back in 2005, he gave me a piece of advice that was so simple and so unwelcome, I wondered if he knew what he was talking about.

He told me to get an office.

I was working from home then, which I liked, and an office seemed like an unnecessary expense. But he was right.

I rented an office and hired an assistant. My stress levels dropped, my productivity went up, and the extra income more than covered the extra expense. Since then, every time I've hired someone, they've made money for me.

One of the toughest things that entrepreneurs have to do if they're to achieve success is to let go. You have to fire yourself from doing the things that you shouldn't be doing. You should be doing only the things that suit you best, the things that bring the most revenue to your business.

The rest you can give to someone else.

Outsource your tasks. Hire employees and freelancers. Form joint ventures with people who can bring skill sets you can't supply yourself. Sometimes, you can even find volunteers who will work in return for free software, experience, or publicity. If you want to grow, you can't stand still—and you can't do everything yourself.

In this chapter, I've tried to reveal the value of your uniqueness, and I've explained the seven keys that you will need to open the gates of your success. In the course of the next five chapters, you will learn the most powerful, proven methods for turning that uniqueness into money on the Web.

Let's begin with the foundation of online success: content.

Content Is Not King . . . It Is KaChing!

You might not be able to hear an actual KaChing sound as you're building an online business, but there is one sound that you'll come across so often it will remain stuck in your head like a bad pop song.

"Content is king."

It's the Internet's chorus, what everyone says when they give advice to new publishers, and what everyone believes as they build a web site.

And they're all right, of course. The Internet is made of content. It's what web sites are built to hold and it's the reason that people open a browser and type in a URL. Internet users surf to learn and be entertained, and they learn and are entertained by digesting content.

What they see will vary tremendously. Some people are just hoping to learn the latest football scores. Others want to read a report that explains why their team lost that match. And some people want to learn why some football tactics generally work better than others so that they can become football coaches.

Whatever you want to find online, whether it's information that's vital and important or trivial and entertaining, and however far you want to take your reading, the Internet is capable of delivering content that tells you what you want to know.

To build an audience online, you have to create content. The better the content, the bigger your audience, and the more influence you'll have over your readers. The more readers and influence you have, the more advertisers will pay to pitch to them, and the higher your click-through and sales conversion rates.

Your ability to earn online then is limited only by your ability to create content that people want. And that's not necessarily just content they can read. Although most Internet content is delivered through words, almost from the beginning, the Web has thrived on its ability to deliver content in all sorts of different ways.

However you deliver your content, as long as it's informative, entertaining, or both, you can build an audience and create value.

In this chapter, I will explain the principles behind profitable content. I'll first discuss how to create content that can generate income, and then I'll reveal no fewer than a dozen different ways to turn that content into cash.

You Don't Have to Be a Writer to Write Valuable Content

This is when people start to get scared. Once they've played around with Blogger or a web site template, they realize that actually there's nothing to creating an Internet site. It's just a matter of checking a few boxes and playing with menus. At the beginning, it all feels very strange and new, but within a few hours, it's as simple as using a pocket calculator.

But the web site only provides a structure. It's as though you've been given a store that contains nothing but empty shelves. You still have to fill it with stock. On the Web, that stock means content—and usually, that content means writing.

There are few shortcuts here. There is free content available that you can put on a web site—things like old books that are past their copyright and now in the public domain, and even old photographs and movies. But such content isn't original, and you'll be competing with all of the other sites offering exactly the same product. You might be able to make a little money with public domain works, but they're rarely the foundation of a successful, ongoing Internet business.

That demands original content . . . and that, in turn, requires original writing.

For people who have never written anything longer than a shopping list, that can sound terrifying. If the thing you hated most at school was writing essays and compositions, if you never got more than a D any time you had to put words on a page and give them to a teacher, I can understand that you're not going to like the idea of putting words on a web site for millions of people to read.

The good news is that writing for the Web is not like writing for school. It's not like writing for college, and it's not even like writing for work.

It's like writing for you.

That's crucial. Obviously, if you're a great wit and can crack jokes and tell killer stories, then you'll have it easy. But you don't have to do any of that. All you have to do is transfer the knowledge that's in your head to the heads of your readers.

So don't try to impress anyone with your writing skills. Don't go flowery or use long words to show that you know how to use a thesaurus. There are no bonus points for pretty writing. There are, however, extra users and additional income available for *clear* writing—and that comes down to two things: information and style.

Of those two, information is the more important, so know what you're going to say before you say it. On Twitter, you can write whatever's going through your head at that particular moment, but when you're writing an article or a blog post, you need to have a plan. That will ensure that every sentence communicates something important and that every word has a use. You won't wander all over the page until you stumble over a good point.

The plan doesn't have to be anything too detailed. It's unlikely you're going to be writing more than 1,000 words—attention spans on the Web are fairly short, and very long posts can put people off—so you won't have to worry about creating long lists of subsections. But you should have an introduction, approximately three points that you want to discuss, and a conclusion.

That's all there is to it. If you aim for each of those three points to run around 300 words, with another 100 or so for the introduction and conclusion, you'll have your article.

If you wanted to write an article for a gardening blog about the right way to choose a bonsai tree, your plan might look like this:

> There are lots of bonsai trees available, so here are some principles to guide your buying choices:
>
>> Climate—There's no point in buying a tree that's going to die in your garden.
>>
>> Shape and size—What look suits your garden best?
>>
>> Care—Do you want to prune and train the tree yourself, or do you want one off the shelf?
>
> Keep these points in mind, and you'll make the right choice.

Now, I don't know whether those points really are important factors to consider when buying bonsai trees. But I do know that this structure is the simplest way to plan effective content on the Web: an introduction, three main points, and a conclusion.

Make the introduction hard-hitting. In RSS feeds and on blog home pages, users will see only the first few lines of the article, and they'll use those lines to decide whether to continue reading. Your opening should be powerful and interesting enough to create the kind of curiosity that pulls readers in. And if you want to make it a little special, try to make sure that at least one of those main points is unique and original. When you're writing on a popular topic, don't just repeat what everyone else has said; give it a unique perspective—ideally, something drawn from your own experience.

Statistics can also help to show that what you're saying is factual and well researched. You can find them on sites like census.gov, fedstats.gov, and the web sites of professional associations. They make your arguments look convincing and give readers solid facts that they wouldn't have known otherwise. Saying that "according to the Nursery Sellers Association, sales of bonsai trees have grown 83 percent in the past four years" adds weight to your post.

That structure is a basic model that you can always call on when you're planning content. You can adjust it for articles of different lengths and add or take away paragraphs depending on the topic. The structure itself isn't important. What is important is that you use one every time you sit down to create new content.

Seven Content Types that Go KaChing

Content can come in many different forms, and all of them have their value and their uses. Here are seven of the most common types of content that you'll come across online, together with their strengths and weaknesses, so that you can choose when and how to use them.

1. HOW-TO ARTICLES

How-to articles are the most direct way to transfer your practical skills to your readership. They're like short manuals that teach a skill. Tim Carter's site is packed full of them, and they don't all have titles like "How to Grout" (although that is the name of one of his videos).

The main strength of these kinds of posts is that if you have the knowledge, they're very easy to write. You simply want to take the readers by the hand and guide them step-by-step through the process of accomplishing the task. The format is largely the same whether you're explaining how to lay tiles, create a layer in Photoshop or perform a cobra in yoga. It's all very simple: Just tell people what they need to do and, ideally, toss in a few pictures to show them. Scatter some ad units in appropriate places on the page, and KaChing, you have profitable content.

As an additional bonus, content like this tends to stay fresh for a long time. A post explaining clearly how to build a deck will be as useful six months after it was posted as the day it was written. Your site won't degrade in time, but will grow increasingly valuable as you add new content.

The disadvantage of how-to articles is that posting a large number of them turns your site into a practical resource. Visitors might stop by when they want to know how to knit a sweater or back up their hard drive, but it's unlikely to form part of their casual reading.

That's not necessarily a problem. Sites like these can still make lots of money. But an online manual might not be the type of site you want to produce.

2. NEWS ARTICLES

News sites are among the most popular on the Web, but they're not necessarily the most profitable. The big news companies like Fox and the BBC already have reporters in place who send back content, so for them, the biggest challenge has already been met and the biggest expense has already been covered. When it's just you, you'll struggle to bring in original content.

There are solutions, though. AppleInsider.com is a news site with no original news content at all (Figure 3.1). It simply aggregates news stories about Apple from around the Web. Anyone interested in following what's happening at the iPhone maker can go to one place and find all the information they want. For the publisher, ads for Macs and iPods will always do well on a site this tightly niched. Alternatively, it's always possible to throw the odd news article into any site and show that it's dynamic and up-to-date.

There are a couple of problems with writing news articles, though. The first is that unless you're breaking the news yourself,

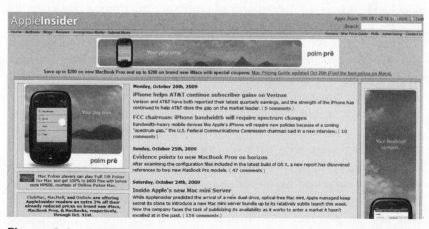

Figure 3.1   AppleInsider.com provides news—and ads—about Apple and the products Apple fans like.

you're going to be rewriting. Cutting and pasting content from a news site is illegal, wrong, and may earn you rude e-mails from lawyers. You'll certainly hear a loud KaChing then, but it will be the sound of your money going *out*. So, you'll have to rephrase the content and state where the information is coming from so that the copyright owners can see that you're not stealing their product.

The second problem is that while news sources are currently free on the Web, it doesn't look like things are going to stay this way for long. News Corporation (owners of the *Wall Street Journal* and a host of other newspapers) has already said that it plans to start charging users in 2010. Other publishers are waiting for News Corporation to make the first move before they bring in their own subscription models. That will make aggregating news on your topic more difficult. On the other hand, it will also make your site more useful to people who don't want to pay multiple subscription fees to different news sites. Best of all, once users are accustomed to paying to read quality content on the Web, they'll be more inclined to pay you for your content, too.

3. OPINION ARTICLES

News articles tell people what's happening. They're at their most valuable when the information you're providing is exclusive or when it's closely related to the subject of your site. But you can make news articles even more useful by combining them with analysis.

This can make all the difference between having just another web site in your field and owning a successful, important web site in your field. Whenever anyone reads the news, the question they always want answered is, "What does this have to do with me?" That's true whether they're watching Fox broadcasters explaining the deficit, a local newscaster reporting on the opening of a new car park, or a sports reporter interviewing a coach. While all of that might be interesting information, viewers want to know whether they're going to be paying more taxes, spending less time looking for a parking space, or getting a piece of information that will help them win an argument in a sports bar. Tell your users why the news is important and what it means to them, and you'll be transforming content that everyone has into unique information and demonstrating that your site is the place to come for expert advice.

For example, in October 2009, the Federal Trade Commission wheeled out a bunch of new guidelines governing the use of testimonials and endorsements in advertising. It was horribly complicated stuff, but it was vitally important to anyone who sells anything online. Anyone with a web site that sold products needed to know about the new rules, so it was no surprise that site after site reported the changes. But what I really wanted to know was what the changes *meant*. What was I allowed to do, and what did I now need to do differently? I contacted my lawyer for advice and, with his permission, shared that advice on my web site. You can read it at www.TwitPWR.com/newftc.

This isn't just a news article saying that the FTC has brought out new rules. There were thousands of articles saying that. This is a professional opinion explaining what that news means, and it's one of the most popular pieces of content on my personal blog.

Clearly, you don't have to ask a professional to explain the news for you—although there's nothing wrong with doing that and many will agree in return for the free marketing. You can also analyze it yourself, giving you another easy and valuable piece of content.

4. REVIEW ARTICLES

Review articles are among the most popular types of content, not because they're easy to write—they aren't—but because they're very easy to monetize.

Create a site that offers reviews of new computers, for example, and you can be sure that many of your users will be people interested in spending thousands of dollars on a new machine. Next to your review of the new Mac, you'll be able to place an ad, and if your readers are interested in making a purchase, they'll be able to click through and spend their cash. Advertisers will be confident enough that it's going to happen to pay you lots of money to tempt people to buy their products. You'll find it very easy to get targeted ads, and you'll find it very easy to convert users into buyers ... provided you can produce good reviews, and that's the tricky part.

When you're reviewing iPhone apps or candy bars, it's not a big deal to spend a few bucks for a solid review. But you won't be able to spend thousands of dollars every time a new flat screen television comes out or each time Apple launches a new laptop. And companies won't send you review samples until your site is an important enough player.

Sometimes, your readers won't expect you to have actually tried the product. If you're enough of an expert, they'll come to your site hoping to read detailed analyses based on the product's specifications. You'll be able to say what should make the new machine better than the last model and what it should be able to do. But unless you've tried it yourself, the review will always be missing something important.

It is certainly possible to make money from a review site based on opinions about new products you haven't actually been able to try—and people do it—but it always feels wrong. When it comes to writing reviews, it's best to review things that you've actually tested yourself. You'll limit the number of reviews you can post, but you'll get much better results, both in terms of your site's reputation and in terms of click-throughs and sales.

5. LIST POSTS

Most of the content you create will be intended to inform and entertain. Sometimes it's also worth creating content to bring in traffic. List posts do that by promising content that can be absorbed at a glance rather than read in detail. Whenever users see a post that promises to reveal "12 Ways to Strip a Car" or "The 43 Most Powerful Left-Handers in Government," they know they're not going to have to work too hard to pick up that information. Each item is going to be just a few lines long, so they'll be able to learn by skimming.

These are exactly the kinds of articles that are most likely to be shared, e-mailed, and recommended on social bookmarking sites like Digg.com (Figure 3.2) and StumbleUpon.com.

List posts require much more work than you may think. In general, the longer the list, the more likely it is to pick up traction and bring in readers. But when you're listing 52 ways to change a lightbulb, you have to do quite a bit of research and creative

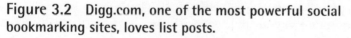

370
diggs

12 Outrageous Ways the Government Wasted Taxpayers' Money
billshrink.com — Spending other people's money rarely compels one to be as prudent as if they were spending their own. Typical politicians are no exception. Look at the ridiculous ways they have spent YOUR money. (Submitted by absolutelytrue)

⌂ digg

📋 78 Comments   Share   Bury   Made popular 6 hr 37 min ago

176
diggs

Gay marriage fight fuels debate over petitioners' rights
latimes.com — The fierce fight over same-sex marriage in California and elsewhere is creating pressure to recognize a new free-speech right that could keep petition signatures secret. (Submitted by entrepreneur75)

⌂ digg

📋 41 Comments   Share   Bury   Made popular 8 hr 7 min ago

241
diggs

WTF? Law in China Forces Kids to Salute Each Passing Car
nytimes.com — Think we've got stupid laws in the US? It's nothing compared to China, where bureaucrats run wild and free. Some examples include the "salute all cars" law mentioned in the title, a law ordering state workers to buy $300,000 worth of liquor per year, a law ordering civil servants to buy 23,000 packs of cigarettes per year, and more. (Submitted by weirdralph)

⌂ digg

📋 51 Comments   Share   Bury   Made popular 8 hr 37 min ago

227
diggs

Koran-Burning rumor sparks anti-American protests
globalpost.com — Shouting "Down with America!" and "Death to the infidels!" hundreds of protesters made their way from Kabul University to the center of the city on Sunday. They were reacting to rumors, vigorously denied by the U.S. Forces-Afghanistan, that American troops had burned several copies of the Koran in a province close to Kabul. (Submitted by Slashered)

⌂ digg

📋 106 Comments   Share   Bury   Made popular 9 hr 37 min ago

301
diggs

Big bonuses, bigger deficits drive waves of populist anger
dailyfinance.com — Americans express conflicting goals: many want more capitalism and less government, while others want a safety net for those who have lost their jobs and their health coverage. Georgetown University historian Michael Kazin, author of The Populist Persuasion, notes that "Big corporations and big government can be seen as parts of the same problem." (Submitted by AmyVernon)

⌂ digg

📋 50 Comments   Share   Bury   Made popular 9 hr 57 min ago

344
diggs

Get Rich Quick: 6 People Who Accidentally Found a Fortune
mentalfloss.com — We've all been there—a week until payday, the rent is due, and you're rummaging in your parents' attic

Figure 3.2   Digg.com, one of the most powerful social bookmarking sites, loves list posts.

thinking to make up the numbers. The post could end up being several thousand words long, taking an entire day or two to write.

It's unlikely that you'll want to include too many of these posts in a blog or web site, if only because they're usually a bit shallow. But toss in one or two a month, and you could find they act as useful traffic bait.

6. Interview Posts

While list posts can be shallow, interview posts are high quality. Because every interview, even if it's with someone who appears regularly on web sites, is different, your article will be unique. And if the person you're interviewing is important and influential in your field, you can be sure that your readers will read it—and see that your site is ready to put in the effort to churn up exclusive content that they can't find anywhere else.

There is a secret to publishing interviews, and it's this: It is ridiculously easy. It looks difficult. It looks as though the publisher has had to go through a whole process of contacting a company's PR firm, setting up a time for the interview, thinking about the questions, researching the subject, and producing piles of carefully thought-out questions. Sometimes it is like that, and the higher the profile of the person you're interviewing, the more hoops you'll have to jump through. Usually though, it's pretty simple.

Call or e-mail the company, explain who you are, and request an interview for your site. Make sure you provide a link so that people can see where they'll appear, and be prepared to provide a link back to their own site in the article. That's the fee that they'll expect you to pay, and it's also a service that you should be providing for your readers. Timing helps here, too. If the interview subject has a product to promote, you're almost guaranteed an interview. You might be put in touch with the company's PR rep (who will handle everything for you), but it's just as likely that the person you're contacting will reply to you directly. The worst thing your preferred contact will do is say no, or not reply at all. That's not a big price to pay. If it is someone in your field, though, and especially if your site has already built a name for itself, there's a good chance that you'll get an agreement.

At that point, you can usually conduct the interview in one of two ways. The first is to set up a time to call. The advantage is that you're in control of the timing. As soon as the interview ends, you have the material you need, and it's just a matter of putting it together and publishing it. The interview will also be flexible. While you'll want to prepare a dozen or so questions in advance, in a telephone interview you can let the conversation wander. That can turn up all sorts of interesting things. Writers often find that they go into a phone interview with one idea for a story they want to write and come out with something completely different—and much better. You'll be able to ask follow-up questions and really dig around.

The downside to a telephone interview is the extra effort. If the person you're calling is in a different time zone, you can find yourself working in the middle of the night. You'll also have to take notes while you're talking, type up a recorded transcript of the conversation (there are tools available that automatically record Skype calls), or possibly both. On the other hand, you'll have built a much closer connection with someone who could prove to be a valuable contact in the future.

The alternative is to do an e-mail interview. That can sound a bit like cheating, especially to journalists used to picking up the phone whenever they need a quote. But when you're building a web site, e-mail interviews can make your life very, very easy. When you prepare for an interview, you're going to be making a list of 10 to 12 questions anyway (more than that and you'll receive short answers in an e-mail), so the work will already be done. People you're interviewing will be able to research their answers and frame them in a way that they believe will make them look good, and they'll be able to do it all in a time frame that suits them. Many of the people you contact will specifically ask for an e-mail interview. Best of all, the interview will be already typed up and almost ready to publish. If you want to run the article in a question-and-answer format, you won't have to do more than a little light editing and ask the subject of the interview for a picture.

The preceding tips apply if you're interviewing someone you don't know. But there's no reason you can't interview someone you *do* know. An interview with a colleague, a friend, a supplier, or a partner can all provide useful, exclusive content, and it's the kind of fun that will make you feel as though you're not working at all.

Interview posts do take a little time to organize, but they really do add a lot of weight to a blog.

7. MULTIMEDIA CONTENT

Most content on the Web is still text-based, but it's become very easy now to post other forms of content. YouTube lets publishers embed its videos onto Web pages, and you can create your own clips and upload them to your site. Photos can also help attract viewers. If you don't want to use your own images, you can pay a buck or so for the high-quality stock images in sites like iStockphoto.com and Fotolia.com or search for Creative Commons–licensed images on Flickr. Just make sure that you tick the box at the bottom of the search page so that you're not breaching copyright. You'll need to credit the photographer and link back to the Flickr page, but in return you'll get a free visual illustration for your article.

Usually, multimedia content forms part of a web site—it's extra content that puts across information in a way that complements the text—but it's also possible to use multimedia as a replacement for text. My site ask.joelcomm.com contains nothing but clips of me answering questions posed by my users and talking directly to the camera (Figure 3.3). They're incredibly fun to do, and you can make the process as simple or as complicated as you want. If you like messing around with editing software, then you can play at being Spielberg and have a blast. Or you can just sit in front of a video camera on a tripod—or even your webcam—shoot, and upload. It's extra, original content in the space of about five minutes.

Those are just seven types of content that you can create for a web site. There are lots of others, but those seven should give you plenty to work with. If you're ever stuck wondering what to post next—and that will happen!—coming back to one of these standard article types should help to break the block.

Figure 3.3　Video content rules at ask.joelcomm.com. Do you see how I turned a how-to post into multimedia content? Serve your content in different formats and you'll reach different types of users.

It's Not Just What You Say, It's How You Say It

So you can put information on your site in lots of different ways. That information will always be the most important aspect of your site, the reason that it will bring in users and succeed—or be ignored and fail. But style plays a role, too.

I'm not going to make too big a thing about this, because the easiest way to destroy any business is to be someone you're not. Whether someone sees me on stage at a conference, tweets me on Twitter, reads my blog, or meets me face-to-face, they're getting *me*. This is the way I am. Not everyone likes it. Some people think I'm too forthright in my views. That's their opinion. I have mine, and I'm not going to try to be something I'm not just to please everyone. That's the surest way to please no one.

When you're creating content for your web site, give it your voice. Don't try to write as though you're creating an article for Fox News or hoping to sell it to *Cosmopolitan*. Picture your best friend in the room with you, and write as though you're explaining what you want to say to him or her. Informality might look strange in the *New York Times,* but it works great on the Web.

That doesn't mean you shouldn't plan what you're going to say. You should still do that. But you should write the way you speak. It's the easiest way to make sure that your site carries your voice and personality and that the content is clear.

Once you've written the article, put it to one side, then go over it before you post. Look for typos, run it through a spell-check, and delete any repetitions. They can make an important difference to the flow. There's a reason reporters will write "Steve Jobs" in one sentence and "the CEO of Apple" in the next. When they repeat the same phrase again and again, the article becomes difficult to read. You want to make the passage as smooth as possible, from beginning to ad click to KaChing.

Ghost and Guest Writers

When you build your first web site, it's likely that you'll be doing most things by yourself. You'll be playing with the designs, bringing in users, and writing the content. That's probably the best way to begin. It might take you a little longer to get rolling, but nothing beats hands-on experience. As you grow, you'll start to look for help, and part of that help can come in the form of writers.

You might find that this happens by itself. When your site becomes well known, other people in your field will ask whether they can put articles on your site. You won't usually have to pay them. They'll get value from the exposure. While that can be good, free content, do make sure that the content is high enough quality. If you lose readers by posting something that's little more than an ad, you'll pay dearly for that post.

You can also hire writers. This is harder than it sounds. The Web is filled with people who think they can write but who actually struggle to complete sentences. You want people you can rely on to produce the content you want, on the topics you want, at the times you want, and at the level of quality you need. Elance.com is one place to look, although it can be pretty hit-and-miss. The feedback ratings should help to reduce the odds of picking a clunker, but don't be afraid to test-drive a few writers and choose the ones you like the best. Alternatively, Scribat.com is a new service that works as both a syndication service and writing agency. You can buy off-the-shelf articles for a set rate, or you can ask the company to commission content for you, in which case Scribat.com will go through the headache of looking for the right people and overseeing the work. You'll just get the content.

Whether you're looking to bring in help from guest writers or hoping to find a reliable ghostwriter to ease your workload, both are legitimate solutions. As long as the content is good—and it will need to be good enough to generate sufficient income to outweigh the cost—bringing in extra writers will help you to grow your online business and allow you take a backseat as it manages itself.

Creating content will always be the main work in an online business. It's what produces the value in your site, and it's what brings in the readers. But content alone doesn't go KaChing. Advertising income does that.

Turning Your Content into KaChing

At one time, monetizing a blog was difficult. Publishers would swear that if they could bring in enough users, those users would be valuable to advertisers. But no one really knew how valuable they'd be or how the advertisers would pay. The result was that advertisers paid far too much money through systems that didn't measure worth accurately ... and the system crashed.

It took a little while for things to get going again, but now we're spoiled with choices. The methods that haven't worked have faded away, leaving only the proven and the most effective channels still in place. In this section, I describe around a dozen of the highest-earning tools that you'll want to put on your web site to generate regular KaChing sounds from your content.

GOOGLE ADSENSE

My initial reaction to using Google AdSense was similar to that of many top Internet marketers.

I thought it was a waste of time.

I'd signed up, pasted the ad code, checked my stats ... and found that I was barely making enough money to keep me in candy bars. I didn't think it was worth handing over large chunks of space on my Web pages in return for little more than a buck a day.

That changed when I attended a small conference in 2004. There were only a couple dozen people there, but one of them pulled out his laptop and checked his AdSense stats right in front of me. I saw that he was making between $200 and $300 per day.

I didn't just hear his KaChing, I also heard a ping as a light went on over my head. I put the code back on my site and started playing with implementation strategies.

I tried different ad sizes. I experimented with the color schemes. I moved ad units to different parts of the page. And I kept track of everything I was doing so that I could see which methods worked best. Within a few months I was making $500 a day, sometimes even $1,000.

I can't tell you how good that KaChing felt!

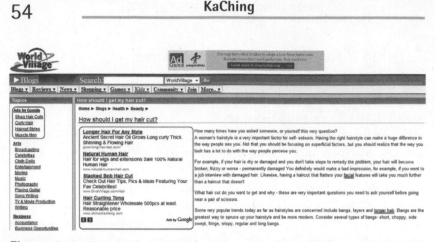

Figure 3.4 Two AdSense units on my site, WorldVillage.com. Look at how I've blended the ads into the page. The link unit on the left looks like part of the site's navigation links; the ad unit in the article is impossible for readers to miss. Careful implementation is key to hearing the AdSense KaChing.

This was everything I'd been waiting for. Ever since I'd launched WorldVillage, I'd believed that the Internet was capable of generating large amounts of stable, reliable—and passive—income to people who were willing to put in the effort to build the sites and figure out how to do it. Here was the proof (Figure 3.4). At the bottom of the daily totals in my AdSense stats were four figures. And it's continued. Month after month, Google has been sending me checks for more than $15,000 each. This isn't some company that doesn't understand the Web, has more money than sense, and won't be around this time next year. This is Google. This is the company that revolutionized Internet search, the company founded by two of the smartest and most technically brilliant people on the planet. This is the company that has actually found a way to keep publishers, advertisers, and users all happy—and make its shareholders happy, too.

I've come across lots of different ways to make money on the Internet, but Google's AdSense has been a reliable source of revenue for me since 2004.

It's a method I can rely on, and best of all, once it's set up and the ads are in place, I can just leave it to do its thing. The money comes in by itself.

When you're building an Internet business, you'll want to fill your site with lots of different cash registers. You'll want to hear that KaChing ring out right around your online store. But you'll also want to think of AdSense as your main cash register. It's the one that can give you your biggest revenues, and it's the one that will give you your most reliable revenues, too.

AdSense is open to just about anyone who wants to use it. The company won't place ads for pornography, gambling, or violent or racist sites—or even sites that sell beer, fake watches, or student essays—but apart from those nasty things, Google will approve just about anyone. You can sign up by clicking the "Advertising Programs" link at the bottom of Google's main page or by surfing directly to www.google.com/adsense. You'll need to identify which domain you want to place the ads on, and within a day or two, you'll receive your approval. You'll then be able to use AdSense's very simple ad creator program to format your ads, choosing the size, color, and other factors that dictate the appearance of the ads. When you're finished, you'll receive a few lines of code that you can paste onto your Web pages that will serve up ads drawn from Google's massive AdWords inventory.

It all sounds very simple. And it is: cut, paste, KaChing.

But if you really want to make the big bucks with AdSense—and there are big bucks to be made with AdSense—you'll want to do a little more than cut and paste. You'll want to understand how AdSense works and what you need to do to make it work for you.

AdSense comes in a number of different forms:

♦ *AdSense for content* is the most popular. This is the kind of AdSense you can see on my Web pages. It displays ads that pay on a cost-per-click (CPC) or a cost-per-action (CPA) basis and that are targeted to the keywords on the page. The ads are usually text-based but they can also be images and even video.

♦ *AdSense for search* provides a search box that you can place on your site. You can specify which sites the user can search, and AdSense will display small text ads next to the results, giving you a share of the advertiser's fee for every click.

♦ *AdSense for mobile content* places AdSense on content built specifically for mobile gadgets like cell phones.

♦ *AdSense for feeds* places ads in RSS feeds, a useful way of making some money from people who read your content in their RSS readers rather than on your site.

♦ *AdSense for domains* lets you make a little money even before your site has launched. Instead of showing a blank page as you're developing your site, you can display AdSense units on pages that contain no content at all. These sorts of pages aren't going to have a great deal of traffic (and Google won't allow you to market an empty page) but it can be a useful net to help you catch visitors to a defunct domain or a work in progress.

If all that isn't enough, *AdSense for mobile applications* lets developers of Android and iPhone apps place ad units in their programs; *AdSense for TV* provides a way for television companies to place ads in the shows they put on the Web; *AdSense for video* monetizes video clips; and *AdSense for games* lets programmers earn money from ads in browser-based games.

Those last four types are available only to "qualified publishers" rather than to just anyone, but it should be clear that Google has a way to place ads on just about any kind of content someone might want to offer on the Web.

In practice, you're most likely to find yourself using AdSense for content and to a lesser extent AdSense for search.

There's little you can do to increase the payments you receive from AdSense for search. You can make sure that the search box is in a prominent place on the page (although users tend to expect to see it in the top right-hand corner), but it's really best to think of AdSense for search as providing an important service for your users . . . that also brings you money. If your users are going to leave and search on Google for their next read, they may as well search from your site so you can earn money if they happen to click on an ad.

It's in AdSense for content that the real work begins. Google can fill content ad units with text ads, image ads, link units, video ads, and gadget ads. If you remain opted in to receive image, video, and gadget ads, you'll get them when they're available and if and when Google thinks you'll make more money with them than with any other unit. You don't get to pick and choose. They do look nice on the page, though: You'll receive a picture or a video—or, if it's a gadget ad, some sort of souped-up, interactive video—and you'll probably be paid on a cost-per-mille (CPM), or cost-per-thousand-impressions, basis. These sorts of ads tend to turn up most frequently on sites with lots of traffic.

You can choose to receive link units. The unit in the top left corner on WorldVillage.com is a link unit. These contain a short list of hyperlinked words. When users click the link, they are taken to a page containing the ads. That means that to earn from link units, users have to click twice. But the unit's small size and flexibility and high click-through rate can make link units great additions to a Web page.

The real workhorses of AdSense for content—and the units most likely to be bringing in the bulk of your site's revenue, at least at the beginning—are text ads (Figure 3.5).

These come in a dozen different formats, and Google also allows you to play with the color and the fonts, which means that you have to do some thinking.

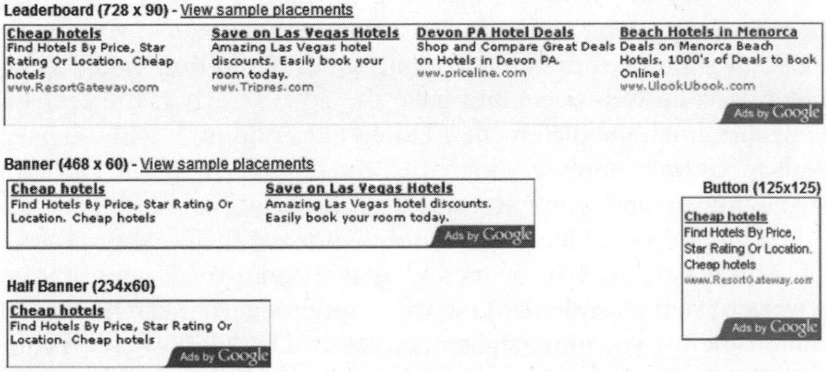

Figure 3.5 Just some of the 12 different formats for text units. There are also 12 different kinds of link units.

The formats you choose, where you place them, and how they look will all determine how much money you earn. Those choices can make the difference between earning pennies per day and making hundreds of dollars per day. It really is that important.

There are some general rules, and Google provides some basic strategies. On the whole, wide formats do better than narrow formats, and the 336 × 280 large rectangle, the 300 × 250 medium rectangle, and the 160 × 600 wide skyscraper are said to be particularly effective.

I wouldn't want to get that specific. Instead, rather than say which formats are best, it's smarter to think about which formats are best for *you*.

AdSense delivers the highest revenues when the units are blended into the page. Users don't visit a web site to see the ads. They come to see the content, and they've now become accustomed to looking around the ads. If they can spot an ad on a page, it's very easy for them to ignore it and focus on the content.

When you disguise the ads and make them look like content, you'll get the highest number of clicks. The user will feel that the links are coming directly from you—and are therefore recommended by you, someone they trust and respect. And because the ads are targeted toward the kind of content you serve, the text will fit right into the site.

One way to blend the ads into the page is to get rid of the borders and match the design of the unit to the design of your page. Make the colors of the ad unit's background and border the same color as your Web page, and have the ad text match the text on your site, and immediately the ad looks like content. It will still have "Ads by Google" somewhere in the box—there's no getting around that—but the unit won't scream, "I'm an ad, ignore me!"

Begin with the blending . . . and then *track*.

This is vital. It's hard work and it takes time. You'll need at least a week of stats to understand what's happening, so it can be several months before you understand completely what works best on your site. But in the meantime, you'll be increasing your earnings and building up some vital intelligence.

To help with the tracking, each of your units should be assigned a "channel," a kind of tag that lets you identify the performance of particular kinds of ads. If you want to know how your leaderboard ads are doing, for example, you could create a channel called "leaderboard" and track the click-throughs and earnings for that channel for a week. You could then swap those ads for half-banner ads and do the same again to see which of the two formats performs best in that position.

There are things that you can't do. You can't encourage your users to click the ads for you. Advertisers will pay for users who like their products, not users who like your product. And you can't click on your own ads, either.

That can be very expensive. Although Google understands that publishers might click on their ads accidentally—and discounts those clicks—if the company believes that a publisher is clicking the ads intentionally to earn extra cash, it cuts them off completely. You'll be thrown out of the system, making it very difficult for you to make any decent KaChing from your web site. There is an appeals procedure, but it's not great. The best thing to do is keep your cursor well clear of the AdSense units on your page. Let your users do the clicking.

The basics of AdSense are very simple. Sign up, format the ads so that they blend into the page, and paste the code onto your site. Test different formats and track the results to see which delivers the best results. It's unlikely that you'll see instant riches. That can happen, but don't expect it. Instead, expect to earn significantly more from your AdSense for content ad units each month than you made the previous month.

When you have the hang of basic AdSense—and are earning the kind of money you always believed was possible on the Internet—you can start getting a little more ambitious. You can start to play around with keywords to find out which subtopics deliver the best ads. You can try AdSense arbitrage—buying users with a keyword on one service and then selling them for a profit through the AdSense units on your own site. And you can start trying to bring in higher-paying video ads and other types of units.

Most important, you can also start to add different kinds of ads to complement the AdSense units on your page, thus increasing the chance that the user will do something to satisfy an advertiser.

For an in-depth look at Google AdSense, and to learn more of my specific strategies, I invite you to download a free copy of my 230-page guide at AdSense-Secrets.com.

KONTERA

Increasing the KaChing from your AdSense units is all about making the ad unobtrusive. But there will always be a limit to how much you can do that. You can't get rid of the little tag that says "Ads by Google," and while you can surround the unit with text formatted to look like an ad unit, that would only harm the look of your Web page. (And Google might not like it too much, either.)

To some extent, users will always be able to spot the ad units on your page. You just have to hope that by the time they do, you've already associated the links strongly enough with your content to leave at least the feel of a recommendation and that the ads themselves are targeted enough to be interesting.

Kontera (www.kontera.com) takes a completely different approach with its ad units (Figure 3.6).

These don't come in boxes that you place all over your Web pages, and they don't come in units. Instead, the code that you place on your site picks out keywords, highlighting them in a different color. When users place their mouse over the keyword, they receive a floating toolbox that delivers the ad. If they click, you get KaChing.

Ads really don't get less obtrusive than this—at least until the user mouses over. The links are completely blended into the text, and that's a huge plus.

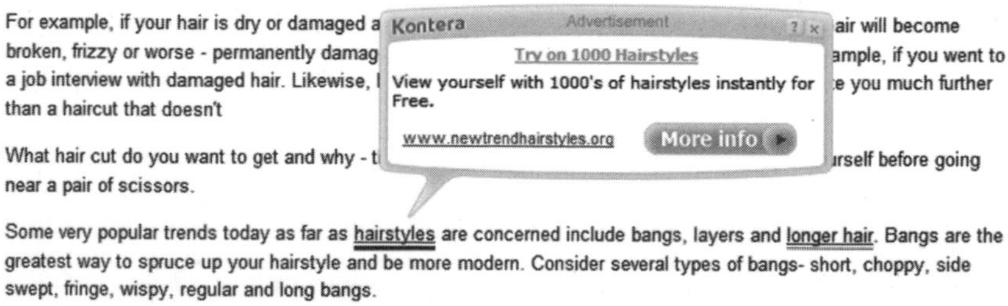

For example, if your hair is dry or damaged a Kontera   Advertisement   air will become broken, frizzy or worse - permanently damag   ample, if you went to a job interview with damaged hair. Likewise, **Try on 1000 Hairstyles** e you much further than a haircut that doesn't   View yourself with 1000's of hairstyles instantly for Free.

What hair cut do you want to get and why - t   www.newtrendhairstyles.org   **More info** rself before going near a pair of scissors.

Some very popular trends today as far as hairstyles are concerned include bangs, layers and longer hair. Bangs are the greatest way to spruce up your hairstyle and be more modern. Consider several types of bangs- short, choppy, side swept, fringe, wispy, regular and long bangs.

Figure 3.6   A Kontera unit in action on WorldVillage.com.

Like AdSense, the units come in a range of different formats—including video ads, flash units, rich media ads, and expandable units that change size when they're played. But you don't get to choose them. Kontera does everything automatically, from choosing which keywords to highlight, to selecting the advertiser, to figuring out which type of ad would suit your site best. (In general, the bigger the site, the flashier the ad.)

That lack of control is a bit of a theme with Kontera. The company provides a small range of tools to help improve your results, but these tools don't do a great deal.

The first tool provides the ability to set the color of the link. Usually, that's very important—and a very easy decision. Users expect links to be blue, so making the links a different color confuses them. If they don't know they can click on it, they ignore it. If you're making money only when someone clicks, you want everyone to know how and where to click, so you want to make your links blue.

Kontera is different. The links do more than take the user to a new page; they also bring up a floating toolbox. Making these links a different color might well encourage users to check them out. They might not click initially, but when just mousing over brings up the toolbox, that could be all you need. Much depends on the design of your site. I've found that blue works best on WorldVillage, but you might find that a different color produces better results for you. Try three or four different colors, track the results, and see what happens.

The other tool is much more important—and much trickier to use. Kontera allows you to mark off certain areas of the page where the ads *won't* appear. Place the line

<span name = KonaFilter>

before the text, and the tag

</span>

at the end, and you won't receive any Kontera ads on that block of text. Clearly, that's a useful way of keeping ads out of your navigation links (where users are unlikely to click on them and where they might interfere with easy browsing), but you can also use them to encourage Kontera to highlight some keywords rather than others.

If a high income on AdSense is all about blending the ad units into the page, on Kontera the loudest KaChing comes when the highest-paying keywords are highlighted on the most eye-catching parts of the page.

Kontera should do this automatically. It should pick out the key-words associated with the best ads. And it should start distributing the ads at the top of the page, spreading them out so that they aren't all clustered at the end of the article where no one will see them. If you want to lend the system a hand by monitoring which keywords are most likely to be highlighted, tracking the amount of money those ads earn and making sure that those highlighted terms appear in short paragraphs and above the fold, then you should find that you get better results.

In practice, doing this for every page on your site could be a lot of work, so you'll probably find yourself working with general prin-ciples rather than strategies for specific pages. For Kontera, those principles for loud KaChings include:

♦ *Keeping the paragraphs short.* Bringing up the toolbox breaks the reading flow. If users see a large block of text, they'll want to reach the end before they start looking around for a diver-sion. Short paragraphs will allow the Kontera link to stand out in white space and provide plenty of natural breaks in which users can bring up the ad.

♦ *Blocking out low-paying areas.* If you can see that ads two-thirds of the way down the page rarely attract clicks, block off that area and keep the ads at the top and away from the navigation bars. It's also a good idea to maintain a safe distance between a Kontera ad and a video unit: The video can block the toolbox.

♦ *Tossing in high-paying keywords.* There's often more than one way to say the same thing, so if you can see that writing "iPod," for example, brings up more effective ads than writ-ing "MP3 player," then use the specific term rather than the general. You'll need to balance this with the need to keep the writing clear, but when you have a choice between two words with similar meanings and different ad values, you'll know which to choose.

Kontera makes a very valuable addition to an AdSense-supported web site. The ads are different enough to provide an extra way to catch more users, and they're simple enough to use to be able to paste, optimize, and forget.

I've arranged for my readers to receive priority treatment from the team at Kontera. Simply visit AdSense-Secrets.com/Kontera.html to apply.

CHITIKA PREMIUM ADS

When Chitika (www.chitika.com) launched its eMiniMalls back in 2005, I was impressed. They were packed with information. Each unit came with a little tab that, when you moused over, gave short reviews or pointed to sites that sold the product. You could see at a glance which outlet had the best price, and you could even scroll through the ad looking for similar items to buy. It was all very sophisticated and very clever. I had great results from them and so did many other Internet marketers.

But there were two problems.

The first was that the ads were really geared toward products. On a Web page that talked about a specific item, such as a computer model or a make of camera, Chitika would perform very well. The ad looked like a widget providing a summary of the main article. On a page that talked about anything else—your vacation adventures, for example, or what you think about health care reform—Chitika's limited ad inventory meant that it was difficult to get relevant ads.

If you had a product site, then eMiniMalls were great. If you didn't, you could safely ignore them.

The second problem was even more serious. Although an eMini-Mall placed on a product site generated lots of clicks—and plenty of CPC revenue for the publisher—it soon became clear that the ads weren't doing a great deal for the advertisers. They were hearing a KaChing, but it was just the sound of the fee they had to pay every time someone clicked an ad. They weren't getting the sales.

This is an important aspect of online advertising, and it's something that's often forgotten.

Users are valuable to advertisers only if they do something when they reach the advertiser's site. Usually that means buying something, but it might also mean signing up for a newsletter—which will lead to future sales—or clicking an ad on their own site. Advertisers won't want to continue paying for users if those users aren't going to pay their way. That's one of the reasons that Google introduced Smart Pricing back in 2005—and it was the problem that Chitika ran up against with the success of its eMiniMalls units.

Users just weren't buying, and advertisers were growing unhappy. If the advertisers went away, then publishers already struggling with Chitika's limited ad inventory would start going away, too.

Google's response was very sophisticated. It began to measure the performance of web sites' users and pay less money to sites with low-value readers. Chitika's was very simple. The company stopped supporting eMiniMalls and created a completely new kind of ad: one that would be shown only to users with the greatest interest.

This is revolutionary . . . and a little unfair. It's as though a store were to close its doors, hang up a sign saying "No time wasters," and allow in only people who were actually going to buy. There are stores that do that, of course. Some outlets work only by appointment. The most expensive shops are designed in a way that puts off people who can't afford the products. Night clubs have bouncers who help create an atmosphere of exclusivity. But on a web site, it's not that simple.

That's because your site isn't the one being exclusive. Your site is still open to anyone who wants to read it. The exclusivity is falling entirely to Chitika and Chitika's advertisers.

Chitika's Premium units appear only to users in the United States and Canada who reach the site from a search engine (Figure 3.7). A user in India or Great Britain who visits your site won't see your Chitika ad. Neither will a regular user—even one based in the United States—if he or she reaches your site directly, instead of visiting it after a search. Those users may see nothing in the ad spot, or they may see an "alternate ad"—a secondary ad that you choose to show when the Chitika ad isn't available. That can be an AdSense unit.

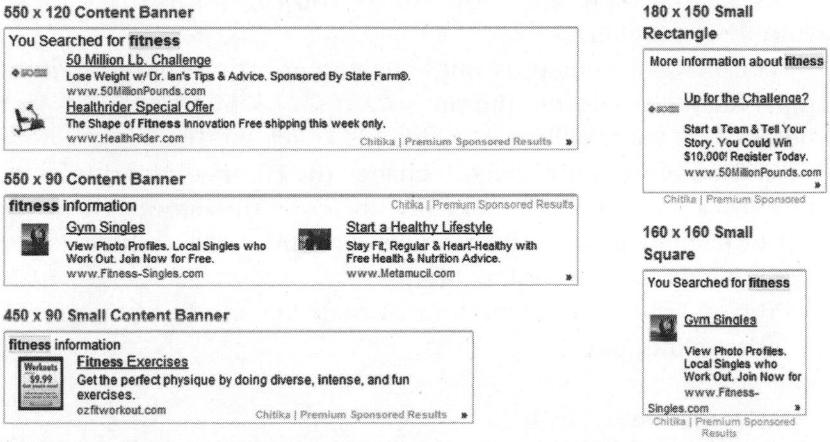

Figure 3.7   Chitika's Premium ads come with pictures and a highlighted search term that make them hard to miss.

If a web site is like a giant mall with cash registers scattered around the floor, ready to pick up money from different kinds of shoppers, then Chitika is the exclusive, posh section at the back of the store. The best shoppers will find a great-looking spot waiting for them; regular shoppers will find a closed curtain ... and you'll have to find another way to monetize them.

To get away with being this selective about its users, Chitika needs to have an exceptional product—and, fortunately, it does. Like the eMiniMalls, the Premium ads look like information boxes. They come with little pictures that attract the eye and have a tab that brings up a search box.

That search box is important. Chitika's selectivity means that it always knows what visitors are searching for. It's able to forget about scanning pages for keywords and looking at meta tags, titles, and subheadings to figure out context. It can simply take the search term and deliver a related ad.

The result is a much wider range of ads than Chitika used to make available, and exceptional targeting. And because users are actively searching for information, there's a greater chance that they'll click on the ad, providing high click-through rates for you and high returns for the advertiser.

As always, there are a few things you can do to make those returns even higher.

The first, of course, is implementation. The usual principles apply: Blend the ads into the site so that they look like part of your content, and users will be more likely to click on them.

Chitika allows publishers to change the colors of the title, text, and URL of the ad link. So make the title color the same as the color of your page's subheadings, the text color the same as the color of your content, and the ad link blue.

You can also change the font of both the ad title and the text with these lines of code:

```
ch_font_title = "Arial";

ch_font_text = "Arial";
```

Again, make the fonts match the fonts on your site. And you can use this line to make sure that the advertiser's page opens in a new window or tab, keeping your users on your site:

```
ch_target = "_blank";
```

That should be pretty straightforward. A little trickier is *where* on the page you should put the units. While ads above the fold always do better than those hidden at the bottom, according to Karla Escolas, Chitika's marketing manager, some publishers have found that placing an AdSense unit at the top of the page and a Chitika unit in the middle generates more revenue than AdSense alone. That's something worth testing.

The real challenge is determining on which pages to put the code.

Chitika reps are pretty clear. They argue that to achieve the best results, the ad code should at least be placed on the site's top five search pages. What you want to know, though, is what kind of ads you want to serve to your most valuable users. Do you want to send your North American search traffic to Chitika's advertisers, or would you prefer them to head to AdSense advertisers, or even your own affiliates? If you know that those other advertisers will always pay more, you might want to avoid putting Chitika units on some pages so that you can better control where those particular users end up.

Again, this is something you'll have to test. You'll probably find that it pays to put Chitika's ads on pages with products but that it pays more to focus on AdSense for your more general pages. Even with the company's wider ad inventory, the best optimization, and the excellent appearance of its ads, Chitika units do look like ads, so they may well be easy to ignore on pages that aren't about products.

In any case, unless you've come across a convincing reason to do otherwise, you should be choosing AdSense as the alternate for your Chitika ads. This is what will be shown to users who don't reach the site from a search engine or who aren't surfing from the United States or Canada.

If those users can't see the Chitika ad, they will at least see an AdSense unit, giving you a good chance of turning them into money.

Another important point to remember about Chitika is that North American users who search on the site can see them, too. If they use a search box that you've placed on your Web pages, that search will be enough to trigger the code.

One very easy way to increase your Chitika earnings is to add an AdSense for search unit to your site and encourage your users to use it to find new content. That should help to turn your regular users into the kind of search traffic that Chitika likes so much. Because you can limit the search results to just your site, you'll be able to keep your users on your pages, while still offering them more ads and creating the opportunity to offer them Chitika units, too.

Chitika is an unusual ad service. It's not interested in converting all of your users, so it shouldn't be used alone. That would mean leaving a valuable part of your web site unmonetized. Nor is it always the best solution, even for the users it takes—but often, it is. When Chitika works, it works very well and, combined with AdSense, it has been known to produce some very impressive results. The challenge for publishers is to place the ads—optimized, with an AdSense alternate, and in the middle of the top search result landing pages—and check the results.

For the right sites and in the right places, Chitika can have a very dramatic effect. You'll want to know if your site is one of them.

Sign up for Chitika Premium at Adsense-Secrets.com/chitika.html.

YAHOO! PUBLISHER NETWORK

So far, all of the programs I've mentioned can work together. Both Chitika and Kontera are at their best when combined with AdSense. They provide another set of cash registers that you can use to pull money from your users. AdSense will always be the main cash desk, but Chitika and Kontera provide useful, additional channels to draw in cash. KaChing can come from lots of different places.

The Yahoo! Publisher Network (www.publisher.yahoo.com) is not compatible with AdSense. You'll have to choose between the YPN network and AdSense. Usually, that's a very simple choice: Go for AdSense (Figure 3.8).

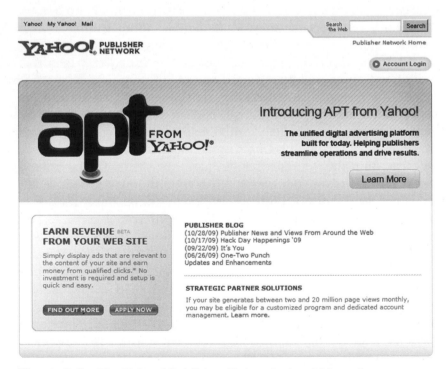

Figure 3.8 The Yahoo! Publisher Network should have been a competitor to Google's AdSense program. It didn't happen.

I wish I could tell you that YPN is a real competitor. I'd really like to be able to say that if AdSense isn't working for you, if it doesn't serve the ads you want or if it thinks you've been clicking your own ads, then you should exercise your power as a consumer and take your business elsewhere. But when that elsewhere is YPN, you really can't.

On the face of it, YPN is exactly the same as AdSense. By purchasing Overture in 2003 for $1.63 billion, the company that had pioneered paid search and inspired Sergey Brin and Larry Page, YPN made its intentions clear. Its ad units look very similar, with headlines, a line or two of text, and the advertiser's URL. Yet YPN has only 10 formats to AdSense's 12, and there are no link units. While you can change the colors of the ads, you can't play with the fonts to improve optimization in the way that you can with AdSense.

Also, the program is open only to publishers in the United States.

That's part of a worrying trend for YPN. The system has always been fairly restrictive, but the tendency now is toward shrinkage rather than growth. In February 2009, Yahoo! shut down its YPN in RSS feeds, one of the few advantages that the system had over AdSense (Google had started offering the same service the previous year), a move that followed the closure of ads in PDF files, another unique offering. The closures seemed to suggest that Yahoo! is focusing on its main products: Sponsored Search and the Content Match ads that make up its AdSense-style ad units.

Unfortunately for Yahoo!, its search engine has only a tiny share of the U.S. search market (just 8.91 percent in October 2009, about the same as Microsoft's newcomer, Bing), and even that share is shrinking. The year before, Yahoo! had been able to pick up just over 12 percent of U.S. Internet searches. That doesn't look good for Sponsored Search, and the prospects for Content Match aren't great, either. In January of 2009, Yahoo! closed the service to European publishers.

Yahoo!'s financial troubles—and its attempts to fend off Microsoft—are no secret, and they throw a bit of a shadow over working closely with them. As the company pulls back its services to focus on the highest-earning parts of the Web, there's always the fear that small publishers may one day be left high and dry. Your ad systems should be the foundation of your Internet revenues, the money you can rely on month after month so that you can experiment with other channels that have higher risks and higher rewards. You don't want to find that one of your most important revenue channels has suddenly been cut off because a company in trouble looks to make more savings.

Fortunately, that's not likely to happen . . . because YPN just doesn't deliver the results that allow most publishers to rely on them. The general feeling among publishers is that Yahoo! delivers poor click-through rates. While the company once made up for that with higher-than-average payments for clicks, those rates have since fallen. The result is that, in a straight comparison, Yahoo! usually performs worse than Google. Its KaChing doesn't ring.

There are things that you can do to improve performance. Implementation, of course, is important, but a big part of the YPN's problem is that its contextualization engine isn't very accurate or very fast. There's a good chance that users will be seeing run-of-network (RON) ads instead of contextualized ads. These are ads that are offered when the system can't decide what it should be serving. They'll have nothing do with your site, and the payments (if you get any at all) will be very low. One way to prevent that from happening and to bring in ads you want is to use "ad targeting."

This is something that's unique to YPN, and it lets you select the advertising categories that you think would interest your readers most. There are about 20 categories and 127 subcategories to choose from. You can even place one page in one category and another page in a second category.

That's a neat trick and a good way to sidestep Yahoo!'s problematic contextualizing, but it's not enough to make YPN a direct competitor for AdSense.

That doesn't mean you shouldn't be aware of YPN or how it works. Google can be very sensitive in its attitude toward click fraud, and its review process can be slow and opaque. If you find—for whatever reason—that you receive one of those horrible messages informing you that your account has been shut down, then you should know that YPN is there as a backup. The formats are similar enough for you to be able to just plug in the new units to fill the space that AdSense left on the pages, but you'll have to work a lot harder—especially with contextualization—before it fills the gap in your income.

MICROSOFT CONTENTADS

Yahoo! should have been the competition publishers wanted to keep Google on its toes. It looks like that space could well be filled by Microsoft (Figure 3.9).

The software company is a relative newcomer to the world of online ads. Its ad units were only seen in the wild for the first time in 2007, a full seven years after Google started placing ads next to its search results.

Microsoft's ContentAds (www.advertising.microsoft.com/publisher) follow the same model as AdSense and YPN. The ads appear in units that can be formatted and optimized, and they are then placed in search results on Bing and across the company's publisher network. For the moment, that publisher network is restricted, and so is the ad inventory.

Figure 3.9 Microsoft tries to out-Google Google with its ContentAds.

Microsoft is currently only accepting publishers based in the United States who have American tax numbers. The company is being selective about who it accepts, and even the ad formats are restricted to 10 different kinds of text ads. There are no image ads, let alone any of the fancy, creative products available from AdSense.

The impression is that Microsoft sees ContentAds as a long-term rival to AdSense. It's building slowly, putting the infrastructure it needs in place as it tries to eat up some of Google's market share.

That's good news for publishers. While it's still too early to tell whether Microsoft really will be able to give Google a run for its money, it's good to know that there is a real alternative. Once your site is up, running, and generating reasonable amounts of traffic, it is worth asking to join Microsoft's beta network. You might decide that you don't want to use it, but you should have it ready if you ever need an alternative to AdSense.

AdsDaq

AdSense, YPN, and Microsoft's ContentAds all deliver CPC ads. (You might get the odd CPM ad with AdSense, but they're relatively rare and tend mostly to turn up on large sites with lots of traffic.) The same is true of both Chitika and Kontera. All of these services rely on users being interested enough in an ad to click on it and head to the advertiser's web site.

That's one way to make money from a site, and it's a very important way. But there are other methods that you can use, and they increase your ability to monetize your users. One of those methods is CPM ads.

Cost-per-mille ads pay a set fee for every thousand times an ad is shown. Usually the payments, measured per user, are very small. Two bucks per mille might be considered a reasonable amount, but it means that you're earning just one-fifth of one cent every time the ad is shown. You'll need to show the ad lots of times to make any decent money that way.

But when you're getting tens of thousands of impressions per day, you will be showing the ads lots of times—and you will be making some nice additional income. Best of all, you won't have to do anything to get that income. To make the most of CPC ads, you have to test different optimization strategies and track the results. It can take time and effort before your ads are really running and earning at full tilt.

CPM ads earn at full tilt the moment they're on your site. As long as the traffic is flowing, the KaChing will keep ringing. And because users only have to see the ads for you to earn from them—they don't have to click, let alone buy—you can put them in the kind of spots that are usually ignored by users. The reason that so many sites have banner ads at the top of the page is that these locations are hard to miss but easy to ignore. Users see them but they don't click on them. That makes the spots poor performers for CPC ads but very useful for advertisers who mostly just want people to know they're around.

When it comes to choosing a CPM network, you're spoiled for choice. There are dozens of networks around that are happy to act as intermediaries, matching web sites to advertisers. Unfortunately for publishers, when it comes to choosing those web sites, those intermediaries are spoiled for choice, too. The result is that many networks have minimum demands for the number of page views a site must generate in order to qualify. Adtegrity (www.adtegrity.com), for example, requires at least half a million page views a month, half of which must come from the United States.

AdsDaq (www.adsdaq.com) is one of the few networks that make no view demands of publishers (Figure 3.10). Even if you're just starting to build up your traffic, you can apply to AdsDaq and start showing CPM banner ads on your site. You won't get much money for them—not until your traffic starts to pick up—but you will get something. More important, you'll get used to having a site that contains another vital moneymaking element, and you'll get a chance to figure out exactly how much your users are worth.

That can be fascinating. When you put an AdSense unit on your page, you have no say in the amount that Google will pay you for that space. If the company decides that a click from your site is worth only five cents, then that's what you'll receive. You won't know anything about it until you check your stats, and only then will you be able to try to block low-paying advertisers and take steps to bring in companies with bigger budgets. In a neat reversal of

Figure 3.10   AdsDaq lets you decide how much you want to earn from your ad space.

AdWords' freedom to let advertisers choose how much they want to pay, AdsDaq lets publishers choose how much they want to receive. (Other networks might do this too, but AdsDaq is rare in that it also has no minimum page views, making it a good place to start.)

Begin with a relatively high amount, say $5 per Mille, to see if anyone bites, then gradually drop the amounts until you start receiving ads. As the site grows, continue increasing the amounts so that you're always receiving the most you can from traffic flow alone.

As you're playing with AdsDaq, you might also notice that the company offers an AdSense-style contextual system. That's something you might want to play with, but don't expect it to perform better than AdSense—or even YPN or Microsoft. The inventory will be much smaller, which means that the targeting will be blunter—and your click-throughs will be lower. On AdsDaq, the CPM ads are the main draw.

MORNING FALLS

Because AdsDaq has no entry requirements, it can be a very useful place to begin. You'll be able to start monetizing those hard-to-promote spots on your Web pages (e.g., the areas at the top and bottom of the screen), and you'll be able to practice checking your CPC stats as well as your traffic-based CPM figures.

As your site grows from a few visits a day to several thousand a day, you might want to think about moving up a level. The reason that CPM networks place restrictions on the size of the publishers they accept is that they want to bring in the highest-paying advertisers. Big companies don't want to have to deal with lots of small sites. They'd rather pay a little more and have their ads seen by the large numbers of people visiting the bigger sites.

As your site grows, generating more money for you and for the ad network, so too does your importance to the network grow. The more money your site is generating for everyone, the more power you have, and the better the service you can demand from the network. While AdsDaq is said to have pretty good customer service, that's not true for all ad networks, especially those with thousands of small publishers. When you're just a name on a list, your request to block an ad category or tighten up the targeting can be pretty easy to ignore. As you move up through the ad networks, though, you should find that the number of other publishers on the network falls and the quality of customer service rises.

Morning Falls (www.morningfalls.com/network) is a step up from AdsDaq. It does have a minimum page view demand, but at just 10,000 unique visitors a month or 200,000 impressions, those demands aren't impossible for even a one-person Internet business to achieve (Figure 3.11).

The implementation is simple, and if you've already been using AdsDaq, it should be reasonably familiar. You can think of the site as a second gear you can use once your site has moved away from the curb and is starting to pick up momentum. Even if the CPM ads that Morning Falls gives you don't actually deliver more income than AdsDaq (though the higher-quality inventory means that they *should*), at least you can gain a little satisfaction from knowing that you qualify.

VIDEOEGG

Once things are really moving, you can think about applying to become part of VideoEgg's (www.videoegg.com) network.

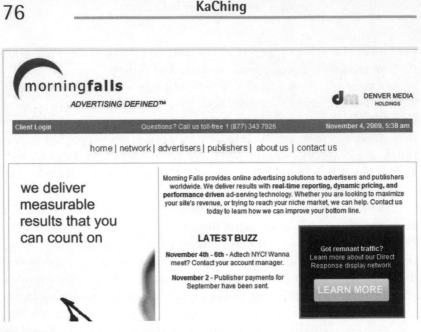

Figure 3.11   Morning Falls takes you just a step higher.

VideoEgg isn't strictly a CPM ad network; it calls itself a cost-per-engagement (CPE) network. It's not entirely clear what that means, but it seems to suggest that the amount you'll receive from running the company's ads on your site will depend on what the users do, not just on the numbers who reach your site, making it more like a CPA system. The least they have to do is to mouse over the little video ad box the network supplies. That turns the box into a much larger overlay, which runs a neat video ad (Figure 3.12).

The ads themselves are beautifully done and generally come from large companies like Lexus, BMW, McDonald's, and AT&T, so you will be showing quality on your site. In return, VideoEgg demands at least 1,000 active users every day. *Active* users likely means users who have actually *watched* the ad, not just passed through a page with an ad on it. You might well need a daily rate of perhaps 50,000 unique visitors to deliver that kind of return.

Clearly, VideoEgg isn't going to be something you'll be putting on your blog as soon as you launch. It might be something you never put on your blog, either because you're happy to stay smaller or because you prefer to stick with other kinds of ads. But it does

This device lets one person hear a voice across the street. But can it stop them from spending too much in an expensive boutique?
WATCH VIDEOS >>

Send this Intervention to a Friend

A *Marshalls* | TJ-maxx Intervention

http://share.videoegg.com/marshallstjmaxx　　　A VideoEgg Experience

Figure 3.12 VideoEgg has some of the coolest ads on the Web. But you have to be big to crack them.

show how far you can go with CPM income. You can start with a small network earning a few extra bucks by placing banners at the top of your page and later find yourself generating really loud KaChings with top-of-the-range video ads served by some of the world's biggest companies.

LinkAdage

An advertiser that pays to put its name on your web site is looking for just one thing: traffic. That advertiser knows that you have the kind of users it is trying to attract, so it's going to pay you to send them in its direction. But there's a second benefit to having a link on a web site, and that advantage isn't the advertiser's, but yours.

Links improve search engine rankings. Advertising doesn't.

Despite the billions spent every year on Internet advertising, the most effective way to bring traffic to a web site isn't ad units, CPM banners, or even affiliate links. It's the kind of links that you put on your site as part of your content because you like what another site has done. Google built its search engine on those recommendations, and those links determine, in part, where a site appears in search engine results.

Win a top spot in those search results for your most important keywords, and you'll get massive amounts of targeted traffic for free.

For publishers, being linked to from other web sites is a vital part of marketing. It's also one of the toughest forms of marketing, so the links have value. Publishers rarely hand out links like these on request; they demand something in return—as you should. That might be something as simple as a return link, but as we've seen, it can also be an interview or even a free article. There are plenty of article banks on the Internet stuffed with free (and generally low-quality) content that publishers can put on their own sites provided they include footer information that usually includes an author bio and a link to the author's own web site. It's an easy and cheap way to spread links around the Web.

There has always been another way to get your link on another web site. You can pay the publisher. If the link isn't being delivered through an ad unit but through an informal deal between publishers and advertisers, there's a good chance that not only will the advertisers get traffic, but they'll also pick up some improved search engine rankings.

When you're looking to make money by selling these kinds of links on your site, there are a number of principles to bear in mind.

The first is that the higher your own search engine ranking, the more valuable the link will be. When a high-ranking site links to a lower-ranking site, that lower-ranking site picks up a massive boost. Sites with a page rank of 6 or 7 will always be able to charge more than those with page ranks of 2 or 3. (There are a whole bunch of tools available on the Web that will instantly tell you your page rank, but the most trustworthy is Google's own toolbar. You can download it for free from www.google.com/toolbar/ff/index.html.)

Like much of Internet business building, the bigger your site grows, the easier it becomes to make money—and the more money you're going to earn.

That sounds obvious, but it's an important point that's often missed. Too many people start Internet businesses expecting to be picking up five-figure checks from Google within a few months of joining AdSense. That doesn't usually happen. It takes time to build content, collect links, improve your page rank, build an audience and create partnerships with advertisers. Link selling might well become a useful part of your revenue stream, but it's unlikely to bring in large sums of money until you have the reputation, the traffic, and the Google love to charge giant amounts.

Selling those links isn't completely straightforward, either. Receiving payments for placing a link on a web site isn't completely black hat, nor is it entirely white hat. The link is going to have two benefits: On the one hand, it's going to help your users reach your advertiser's web site. That's legitimate. Every link does that, and Google, after all, has become a multi-billion-dollar company by helping companies do this. Selling links directly simply cuts out the intermediary and lets you pocket the entire fee.

But the link is also supposed to help advertisers improve their own search engine rankings, and that means deceiving Google, at least a little. Google will raise the advertiser's ranking because it believes that you've supplied the link after seeing something on the site you like. You approve of the site, you think it's something your users should know about, so you've told them the site is worth visiting. That tells Google the site is important, so the company tells its searchers that the site is worth visiting, too.

If Google knew that the other site had paid you for that recommendation, it wouldn't count it. Google does have a way of discounting some of the links that sites receive. A link can be categorized as "dofollow," and Google will count it, or "nofollow," and Google won't. Links placed on Twitter, for example, are generally "nofollow."

I could tell you that it's unlikely that Google is going to suddenly declare all of your outgoing links "nofollow" and take away an asset that you can charge for. And I could suggest that when you're dealing with another site directly, you really should only be accepting links from sites you know and trust.

But in practice that's not the way things work.

If another publisher asks you directly for a link, then you should either supply it for free—as part of your content or, more usually, a link exchange—or you can offer to sell that publisher advertising. If you're looking to sell space for text links to sites you're not familiar with, then there are number of services that act as brokerage houses.

Even eBay has been known to list text link space, although the results have usually been pretty poor: Advertisers have paid and received nothing in return.

LinkAdage (www.linkadage.com) is at least reputable and reliable. You can set your own rate for a link, or you can create an auction, ensuring that you receive the best price possible. Typical prices range from $70 to $275 a month for a site with a high page rank. LinkAdage will take a 50 percent fee, however.

COMMISSION JUNCTION

Text link ads used to be very helpful. These days they've largely been overtaken by contextual ad systems like AdSense or Chitika. When you're just starting out, those companies will serve up relevant ads very easily. And when you're established enough to have the sort of page rank that makes selling links worthwhile, you'll want to think carefully about doing so. You'll be linking to the most important sites, anyway, so any link you receive is likely to be a relatively minor site. You might find that it's just not worth the fee.

That doesn't mean you should never do it. You'll just want to weigh the benefits of an additional couple of hundred bucks against the costs of placing links to a site that your users might find disappointing.

More traditional—and more useful—are cost-per-action (CPA) ads. While CPC ads pay solely for a click, and CPM ads pay only tiny amounts every time the page is loaded, CPA ads pay when the user does something the advertiser considers valuable, such as completing a form and becoming a lead or making a purchase.

If that sounds like affiliate advertising, then the idea is exactly the same. I'm going to talk in detail about earning affiliate income later in this book, but there is one vital difference between affiliate advertising and CPA advertising with the help of an agency.

Sign up with a CPA ad agency and you'll have no idea which ads you'll be serving. While it's true that you'll always have some measure of control—you should be able to block companies you don't want, and you might be able to pick categories of products you prefer to advertise—the real benefit of using an agency is that you don't have to do any of that stuff. Once you've signed up, you're making your site available for advertisers to choose you.

Figure 3.13 Commission Junction is among the heavy hitters of CPA advertising.

The fees vary tremendously, but because CPA ads are popular with some very big companies that tend to pick large sites for their distribution, if you can deliver the traffic—and the action—they can give you a pretty nice KaChing.

Lots of different agencies can send CPA ads your way, but one of the most reliable is Commission Junction (www.cj.com) (Figure 3.13). The company now forms part of ValueClick, which bought it for $58 million in 2003. (I always said online advertising pays.)

Commission Junction has some nicely detailed stats and some very big names in its advertising networks. You could find that your site is advertising Dell, Yahoo!, Expedia, or HP. Those are the kinds of companies that make your site look good—and win clicks from curious users.

That's a big advantage.

For top-earning publishers—those making more than $10,000 a month from their Commission Junction ads—the company offers a special service with a dedicated account manager. For advertisers, Commission Junction offers different levels of participation (including appearing in search results), which makes it a good place to start, as well as to build a large-scale campaign.

It should be clear that once you've created your content, there are lots of different kinds of ads that you can place around it. Contextualized CPC ad networks like AdSense, YPN, and Microsoft's Content Match, will "read" your pages, serve ads that match the subject, and pay you fees that range from a few cents to tens of dollars for each click the ads receive. Other CPC networks, like Kontera and Chitika, offer additional ways to do the same thing, blending their ads neatly into your page and increasing the chances that you'll win those clicks.

CPM ads, like those supplied by AdsDaq will pay for your traffic regardless of what your users do, while CPA networks will give you larger amounts, provided your users actually do something. You can even sell text links directly, either by yourself or through a network like LinkAdage.

If that sounds complicated, understand that in practice it's very simple. Start by placing AdSense on your site. Add Kontera, and if you think it will suit your content, Chitika, too, using AdSense as the alternate. Take the time to optimize and track your AdSense results, and while you're doing that, also build up your traffic so that when you place CPM ads, you're making decent money.

Over time, you'll find yourself discovering which ad formats deliver the most clicks. You'll come to see which topics deliver the most value. And you'll start to build up the kind of traffic that makes banner ads worthwhile.

Again, this won't happen overnight. While you should be able to see some income right away, it might take several months before that income is enough to repay you for the time and effort you're putting in. But if you're persistent and determined, if you're prepared to learn, experiment, and adapt, you'll get there. Your web site will be generating up to a dozen different types of KaChing from content alone.

But content delivered for free on a web site and supported by ads isn't the only way to make money with the knowledge you possess. In Chapter 4 I explain how to earn the full value of your expertise . . . by selling information products.

Information Products—Selling Your Knowledge

All of the methods that I've described so far have been based on the idea that the knowledge you possess has value. Whether you've picked up that knowledge from years of practicing your profession or learned it by indulging in your passion, if other people want to know what you know, you have an opportunity to make money.

Everyone has knowledge like that. Everyone can now build a web site to display that knowledge. As we saw in Chapter 3, there are now plenty of different ways to surround that knowledge with advertisements, giving you a steady stream of revenue. You don't even have to go out and track down the advertisers yourself. Google and other services will serve them up automatically, matching their inventory to your topic.

As long as you're adding content, bringing in readers, and tweaking those ads until they're working at full power, you'll be hearing KaChing.

An ad-supported content site gives your knowledge away for free. You can make a lot of money with it, but that money doesn't

83

come from the value of your knowledge. It comes from the value your readers have for your advertisers. If your users like to buy lots of things from your advertisers, you'll make lots of money. If they prefer to read and click away without touching an ad—and some traffic sources have lots of users like that—then you'll struggle.

In the meantime, you'll have given away something valuable of your own for little reward.

You might think that there's no other way. For years, we've been hearing that it's impossible to get people to pay for content online. Everyone has become so used to being able to read the news for free, browse magazines for free, even watch movies and listen to music for free that trying to persuade Internet users to part with cash is like trying to get teenagers to clean their rooms: It's something you know you should do, but why waste your time when you know it's never going to happen?

The reality is very different. In fact, when the incentives are in place and the product is right, not only is it possible to sell information online, but you can actually get closer to the real value of that information.

That's something that's very difficult to do offline.

Head to a movie theater, for example, and you can expect to pay about $10 for a ticket. The price might vary slightly, depending on the location, the plushness of the theater, and whether the movie is in its first run, but no theater is going to expect you to cough up $50 or $60 for a ticket. The ticket price a theater can charge is fixed within a fairly narrow band.

Whether you're seeing an 80-minute comedy that leaves you cold or sitting spellbound through a three-hour sci-fi epic, the price is roughly the same. And that's true even though you might come out of the epic aware that you would have been willing to pay three or four times more for that experience.

In order to squeeze more money out of the movie-going public and reduce the gap between the price of the ticket and the value of the experience to the moviegoer, movie companies have had to get creative. They've had to offer features with clear additional value, such as Technicolor, surround sound, or IMAX. They release DVDs packed with special features and offer merchandise to children to squeeze every penny they can out of the value the movie has to the audience. Just calling it an "epic" or adding half an hour to the film won't do the trick.

In the publishing world, the limitations for sellers—and the opportunities for buyers—are even clearer. One of the best-selling books in 2009 was Ramit Sethi's *I Will Teach You to Be Rich*. Describing itself as a six-week financial boot camp for 20- to 35-year-olds, the book explains how to automate savings and investments, negotiate raises, manage student loans, and generally be smart with money. If it does what it says it does on the cover—and there's no reason to believe it doesn't—then over the lifetime of the reader, the knowledge in that book should be worth hundreds of thousands of dollars. Ramit Sethi should be able to sell it for thousands of dollars a copy and still call it a bargain. You can buy it on Amazon for less than 10 bucks, making it perhaps the best investment this side of Wall Street.

The book sells for that price because it's a paperback, and that's what paperbacks sell for, especially after Amazon has done its price slashing. Buyers don't look at the value the book contains for them but at the price of the next book along the shelf. When the competition is that fierce—and price expectations so low—publishers have little choice but to pitch their books in the range that the book-buying public expects.

Move away from long-established and tightly priced industries like movies and publishing, though, and sellers start to enjoy more freedom. In addition to selling a *New York Times* best-selling book, Ramit Sethi also runs virtual boot camps that build on his book's content by providing Q&As, webinars with other financial experts, and information about "entrepreneurship and psychology." These are not very different from the content of his book, but because they're not in book form, Sethi can charge a price closer to their real value. The boot camps cost $199 and sell out quickly.

The Internet is such a new marketplace that information products sold online can enjoy plenty of pricing freedom. Copywriter David Garfinkel, for example, sells his copywriting kit online for $997. Buyers get more than a book, of course. They receive a stack of DVDs showing a complete seminar that students have paid thousands of dollars to attend, together with transcripts and audio versions.

It's all valuable information, but it's presented in a way that allows Garfinkel to cram in more details than he could in a 200- to 300-page book—and also allows him to charge a price closer to the amount that buyers can expect in returns on their investment. While $997 might look like a lot of money for a pile of DVDs, buyers realize that one sales letter they write using the information they paid just under a thousand dollars to learn could easily offer them 50 or 100 times that amount in return.

The format the information comes in no longer matters. Only the value of the information matters. Create information products, and you'll be able to realize the true value of your expertise. That can mean hundreds and even thousands of dollars for every sale.

In this chapter, I explain how to create information products. I explain how to come up with killer ideas, create the product, write the copy that turns browsers into buyers, and recruit affiliates. I even discuss the most important practical steps, such as creating shopping carts, fulfilling orders, and of course, giving your product a rocket-powered launch.

Creating Killer Ideas for Your Information Products

I started this book by talking about creating a content site. I think that's always the best place for any Internet business to begin, because it's the easiest. You don't need any special skills to create a web site, fill it with content, and surround that content with ads.

Once you hear that KaChing sound for the first time, you'll immediately receive a massive injection of motivation to keep going and to make that KaChing ring louder.

But there's another reason I think that it's a good idea to start with a free, ad-supported web site. As you're writing content, reading comments, and talking with your readers on Twitter and Facebook, you'll also be getting an idea of who they are . . . and what they need.

That's incredibly valuable information.

Put up a blog post that no one reads and you'll have wasted an hour, maybe two. But you'll also have helped your site's search engine ranking and learned something about what your audience *doesn't* want to see. You'll have risked little and won a little. That's the worst-case scenario, and it's really not terrible.

But creating information products does require a larger investment. As you'll see, there are ways to reduce the risk without significantly affecting the returns, but the risk that you'll lose time or even a little money creating an information product that doesn't sell is always higher than the loss you might endure by creating a dud blog post. Three factors will decide whether your information product makes a giant KaChing or a dull silence: the idea, the implementation, and the launch.

The idea sounds like the hardest part of the product. It looks like it's the most important and the toughest to get right. You need to do lots of research, test the ground, carry out surveys, and build focus groups. Get it wrong and you'll never see a dime for your efforts, your product will fail, and you'll have to stay at your *job* for the rest of your life.

Actually, none of that is true, and while you might want to do a bit of research before you get to work, you won't have to do too much market testing before the release. You're creating an *information* product, not a new flavor of Coke. There might be some risks associated with information products, but the costs are low . . . and the brainstorming is very simple.

The first rule in choosing a topic is to follow your gut.

If you've created an online business in a field that you enjoy, that you understand, and that you've already spent time in, you should have a feel for the market. Your customers will be people like you, and you'll have a sense for what you—and others with your interest—would be willing to pay to learn.

That doesn't mean you should rush out and create the first information product you think of. If you've thought of it, there's a good chance that someone else will have thought of it, too. You'll certainly want to make sure that the product you're thinking of creating isn't already available and that there is room for your own take on the subject. Looking at those other titles will also give you an idea of what's selling and what the market is used to seeing. All of that is important.

That's straightforward enough, but though your sense for your subject can point you in a general direction, it's not enough by itself to plot your course. You will also have to do at least *some* research.

And that leads to the second rule of information product brainstorming: Listen to your readers.

As a web site publisher, your readers are both a vital part of the market and a market that talks to you. The comments they leave at the end of your blog posts and the actions they take on your site give you tons of valuable information about what sort of information they might (and might not) be willing to buy.

The comments themselves are obvious, but they're also unreliable. It's possible that some users will say specifically that they'd be prepared to pay for a book that would tell them how to build their own patio or how to cook dinner parties in a snap, but you can't rely on those kinds of posts to tell you what information product to create. What you can do is look at the number of comments your posts receive to see which topics push people's buttons the most. Although there's a difference between prompting people to write a comment and driving them to spend money, it is likely that controversial topics will help you to move more goods. The comment count will help you to identify the subjects most likely to generate interest among your users.

Comments are the most obvious sources of information about your user preferences, but they're not the only intelligence that you can use to make smart decisions. Your web site stats will also tell you which pages are the most popular and how long users spend on them. That's a measure of interest. If a blog post topic has generated lots of views and persuaded your readers to stick around and read through to the bottom of the page, that's a good sign that people are gripped by the subject. There's a reasonable chance that they'll find it interesting enough to pay to continue reading.

As you're wondering what sort of topic you should use for an information product, take a few minutes to look at your site stats. List the 10 pages that generate the most views, the 10 pages that generate the most comments, and the 10 pages that generate the longest views. You should find that there's plenty of overlap, giving you a good idea of what attracts your readers the most.

Those figures will tell you how much interest your readers have in the topic before they reach your page. They won't tell you how much interest remains *after* they've read your page. While it's unlikely that a single blog post will be enough to completely satisfy people who want to know about a topic, it's certainly possible that a good post will leave them feeling that they know enough not to need to read more. (That's not a reason to write poor posts, though. If one post can satisfy readers, then the topic is too narrow for an information product.)

However, you do have a measure that tells you how much interest remains after someone has read your post. Your ad stats don't just reveal how well your ad units have been optimized, they also show you that having read your post and looked at your page, your readers still want to learn more. They've clicked the ad to continue their education. That tells you there's a demand that still hasn't been met.

When you've listed the posts and topics that have attracted the most views for the longest amounts of time, add the pages with the highest click-through rates.

All of these figures will give you a sense of the demand for your expertise. But they won't give you an answer to the question, "What should I create an information product about?" They'll give you areas to think about. They'll inspire you. But you still have a couple more things to throw into the pot.

Your information product should be on a topic you know well and can talk about intelligently. There's no point in choosing a subject that you think your audience would pay for if you don't actually know more about it than they do.

And it has to deliver results.

That's the really crucial bit. When you're asking people to pay you money for information, they're only going to reach into their pockets if they believe that money is going to come back to them. That doesn't have to be in cash form—although you can certainly find plenty of information products on the Web that promise to help people earn giant stacks of cash—it can also be money saved.

Create an information product that explains how to build a deck, for example, and you'll be able to tell people that they're saving the labor costs involved in hiring someone to do the work for them. As long as you're charging less than the amount that a buyer would have had to pay, you'll be offering a bargain. Your buyers need to feel that they're swapping the cover price for a later return of money or some other benefit.

I wish I could tell you that there's a fail-safe formula for coming up with ideas for information products. I wish I could walk you through the process of reading your server stats and ad stats until the opportunities leap out and grab you. And I wish I could claim that if you do all of these things, check the market, and outline the value your product brings that you're guaranteed to make a profit.

But I can't.

When you're creating information products, there are no guarantees. There are gambles of various odds and risks with different levels of reward. But there are also ways of reducing the risk, and there are so many opportunities available that the biggest risk you can take when building an online business is not creating an information product at all.

Creating the Product

What kind of product do you want to create? A book? An e-book? A set of DVDs? Or how about a subscription-based virtual classroom that, over the course of several months, teaches your customers everything they need to know to complete their goals?

There's no one way to create an information product. Instead, there are a number of different ways of transforming the information you have into a format that can be sold online. For the buyer, the format itself doesn't matter. As long as the information is able to flow efficiently from you to them, they'll be getting their money's worth. But what the different formats *can* do is affect *how* that information is transferred, *how much* information is transferred—and how much you have to invest in creating the product.

E Is for Easy ... and E-book

The easiest approach is to write an e-book. This is how I started creating information products and the result just blew me away (Figure 4.1).

After I'd seen what AdSense could do, I got in touch with a few friends and told them what I'd discovered about optimizing ad units.

Figure 4.1 The first edition of my AdSense Secrets e-book was about 60 pages long ... and I sold thousands of copies at $77 each.

A day after trying out some simple strategies for himself, Chris Pirillo, creator of blog network Lockergnome.com, got back to me with the single word: "Dude!" Dave Taylor (AskDaveTaylor.com) and tech guru Bob Rankin (TheInternetTourbus.com) were also enthusiastic, and soon I was telling everyone I met that they needed to be shaking up their ads, blending them into the page, and testing different formats.

At that point, someone suggested I put the results of my experiment in an e-book and share it online.

I didn't know anything about information products then. I'd never created one, and much of the content on my web site was being provided by volunteers and professional writers. I was contributing only occasionally, so the idea of sitting down and writing an entire book didn't appeal to me a great deal.

But I wanted people to know this stuff. I'd wasted a lot of time and lost a lot of money by not optimizing my ads, so the sooner people understood what AdSense could do, the sooner they could earn real cash, too. Of course, I wasn't completely altruistic, either. The more people who used AdSense, the more advertisers would like it, the more ads there'd be online, and the more money there'd be available for everyone. That's one of the great things about AdSense: The larger the competition, the greater the opportunity.

I was also going to charge for it. If people were going to take my research and make money, then I was thrilled for them, but I couldn't see why they should object to paying me for helping them make that money.

So I did it. I took the same approach to the book that I take with anything that I put up on my sites: I forgot about being literary and trying to talk like a newspaper, and wrote the way I speak. It seemed the easiest way to do it, and I couldn't really see myself doing it any other way. I pretended that I was on the phone with one of my friends explaining the results of my AdSense testing—something I'd done many times.

What Google Never Told You about Making Money with AdSense came out in February 2005. It was about 60 pages long—short for a book, but plenty long for an e-book. Most important, it contained everything I had then learned about AdSense, so I wasn't too concerned about the length. I knew that if readers implemented the strategies in the book, they'd make money. Those strategies had made money for me, and they'd made money for friends who had used them. I didn't think that buyers would care that they had to read only 60 pages rather than 300 before they could improve their income.

I priced the e-book at $77.

For a book, that's a giant amount of cash. The only books you'll find for that sort of money in your local Borders will be double-sized, limited edition photo books with hard covers and glossy pictures. Most of that money will be spent on printing.

My e-book was digital. I didn't have printing costs and I didn't have distribution costs. I would have affiliate costs, though. Sellers could be taking as much as half of the cover price as a commission, but that would still leave me with almost 40 bucks for every sale, which seemed like a nice amount. For strategies that had improved my income from a buck a day to 1,000 bucks a day, it was a steal.

I had no idea what was going to happen when I started selling. My guesstimate was that I might make an extra $1,000 a month. For an e-book that was meant to help other people make money, that would always be fine by me.

Of course, I didn't just put the e-book on a web site and tell my own web site users about it. I also got in touch with some big affiliate marketers and offered the book to them. One of the first to sign up was Paul Myers, whose TalkBiz.com web site had already made him famous as an affiliate marketer. Paul mentioned the book to his subscribers . . . and sales, helped by this network of affiliate sellers, rocketed.

That $1,000 a month that I'd been expecting turned into $10,000 in just two days.

An e-book priced at $77 was flying off the servers. Not only was it clear that it was possible to price even short documents far higher than you could get in the stores, it was also clear that affiliate selling helped move them and that people were prepared to lay out real cash for a book that promised to return that money if its strategies were implemented.

It also proved to me that creating e-books really isn't difficult. The book itself hadn't taken me very long at all to write, placing it on the servers was a breeze, and best of all, once the setup was complete, the money rolled in by itself.

Since then, I've updated the e-book four times, adding more information, discussing more strategies, and extending those original 60 pages to more than 200. I even raised the price to $97 for the second and third editions! These days, having made tens of thousands of dollars from that e-book, and with much of the information contained in it now being shared among Internet marketers, I give it away for free. You can pick it up at www.adsense-secrets.com.

When I say "free," I don't mean entirely free. To download the e-book, you'll need to supply your e-mail address. I don't sell those addresses or let anyone else use them, but it does help me to build up a list of people interested in creating an online business. In return, I also send readers my weekly online business newsletter, another way to deliver value and to let entrepreneurs know about any other products I have to offer that might help them.

Creating an e-book is simple enough. The document should be in PDF format, which makes it easy to distribute while still offering plenty of formatting options, an attractive, booklike appearance, and a relatively small file size. While you can—and should—pack pictures, graphs, and images into your e-book to break up the text and make it inviting to flip through, remember that all of those extras will increase the book's weight. That means that it will take up more space on the server and take longer to download. You really want to keep the weight below five megabytes. If you go over that, start looking for pictures to take out.

You can create the e-book using Adobe's own Acrobat program. That's probably the best way, and if you were to hire a designer to lay out the book for you, that's probably how he or she would do it. But even the simplest version of the software costs about $300, and since you're only going to be using a fraction of the features you'll be buying, it might not be the best move. Instead, you can write up your document using Word (or even a free word processing program like Open Office if you're really strapped for cash) then convert it to PDF. Adobe itself lets you do that from its web site at www.createpdf.adobe.com. A subscription that enables you to convert as many documents as you want costs from $9.99 a month, but you can start with a trial run of five documents.

In other words, you can create PDF versions of your first five e-books for free. Once you've burned up those five samples, you can either pay 10 bucks for your next e-book . . . or download PrimoPDF, a free program that does much the same thing.

The book itself doesn't have to be anything too complex. While pictures and graphics will make the book easier to read and appear more professional, they're not strictly necessary. If you can do it, then your readers will appreciate it, but if you're no designer and don't want to pay for one, then you can skip those extra bits and focus only on the text. Your customers will be paying only for the information and, more important, what that information is going to do for them. If a design element looks good but doesn't actually contain information that will help buyers achieve their goals, then you don't have to sweat too much about leaving it out if you're struggling to work it in.

What you should include are a table of contents so that people can see what the e-book contains, page numbers so they can find the information they want quickly, and a footer with a link to your web site.

That's crucial. In theory, no one should be able to read your e-book without having paid for it first. In practice, your e-book is going to fly around the Web and be seen and used by all sorts of people who didn't pay for it. The more popular your book, the more valuable it is to your market and the more people are going to pass it to their friends. While you should send rude e-mails threatening legal action to anyone *selling* your e-book without your permission, you'll gain very little by raging against those who share your file for free. Including a link to your site on every page will let you offer more products, and ads, to every reader—even the ones who didn't buy.

As we've seen, the length of an e-book can vary. Anything longer than a blog post can be turned into a PDF document and made available for download without users wondering why they can't just read it in their browsers. Once you get to about 3,000 words, you're either going to have to break up what you want to say into different pages—which gives you more opportunity to serve ads—or put it in a PDF e-book and let people download and read it when they want. You can find plenty of very short documents of even 10 to 12 pages on the Internet calling themselves e-books. Those kinds of very short documents are best used for viral marketing. You can offer them for free to people who sign up for your RSS subscriptions, or you can just distribute them as additional content that shows the value of your information. As people share them and talk about them on their own web sites, they'll send you some useful extra traffic and help to brand you as an expert.

When you're looking to *sell* an e-book, you'll really want at least 50 pages. That's still much shorter than any book you'll find in a bookstore, but perceived value does still have an effect on sales. Fewer than 50 pages and customers will begin to wonder whether the e-book will contain enough information to have a meaningful effect on their lives. That's the impression you're always looking to create.

The same is true of maximum length. For print books, the more pages the book contains, the higher its apparent value. That holds true online as well, but be aware that when an e-book gets very long—more than 200 pages, say—readers stop reading and start dipping. They look at the table of contents for the particular information they want, turn to that section and pluck it out. There's nothing wrong with that as long as they're still buying the book, but if you are writing something very long, try to break up the sections so that they can stand independently. It's likely that many of the people reading Chapter 7 of your e-book won't have read Chapter 5.

When it comes to length, you have all the flexibility you could want. When it comes to pricing, you have more flexibility than you could want. If customers are prepared to pay $77 for a 60-page e-book about AdSense what would they pay for your e-book?

It would be great if you could price the book in the same way as any investment. If you knew that people implementing your strategies were going to add $12,000 to their income at the end of 12 months, then you could charge $1,000 and tell people that they'll get their money back within a month.

But it doesn't work that way.

While you can estimate what someone might make by implementing your strategies, you can't predict their future earnings. Everyone will act differently, grow at different speeds, and see different levels of success. Try to claim a typical rate of return, and it's just possible that you could even have the Federal Trade Commission on your back. More realistically, buyers won't believe you. They understand that the amount they can earn after buying your e-book will depend on what they do with it. Charging a high price on the basis of predicted earnings could result in fewer sales.

So, be modest . . . and look at the competition.

Even though your product should offer unique strategies, plans, and ideas, it's unlikely that you won't have any competition at all. You should read those other e-books that are available in your field to see what they contain, understand how the authors arranged their ideas, and stay up-to-date. Pay attention to the pricing of those books. If you charge twice what your competition is demanding for a book that also promises to help people make money as fashion designers, create a top-selling Etsy store, or save thousands by building their own kitchen, then you'll need to show that your e-book contains something that delivers twice as much value.

Otherwise, your targeted readers will be able to buy the same benefits from your competitor at half the price.

While your competition will limit your ability to set prices, at least a little, they do make coming up with a figure a lot easier. (And don't forget that you'll be giving away a large chunk of that income to your affiliate sellers.)

So when you're looking to sell your knowledge, you'll want the e-book to be at least 50 pages. You'll want it to contain solid, practical information that delivers real benefits. And you'll want it to be priced in line with the competition rather than relying entirely on the perceived benefits the book will bring.

That should be enough to give you a simple information product that can deliver a steady chorus of KaChings.

GETTING PHYSICAL WITH PRINT BOOKS

When you can create an e-book that's as short as 60 pages, charge as much as $77 for it, sell thousands of copies, and do it all on your own terms, according to your own schedule, and without having to ask anyone's permission first, why would anyone want to create a print book?

That was the question that went through my mind when David Hancock, a former mortgage banker and the chief executive of New York publishing company Morgan James, suggested turning my e-book into a print book that would be published and distributed in traditional hard- and soft-cover versions through his firm.

We had met at a conference, and although we'd hit it off right away and I was flattered by his offer, my initial reaction was skeptical. The e-book was selling well. In fact, it was selling better than I could have hoped. Producing a print book would mean reorganizing the content, and worse, it would also cap the price. It's unusual for a book to sell for more than $25 or so, and authors are usually last in line to get their share. By the time the retailer, publisher, and printer all have their take, traditional authors are usually left with a tiny fraction of the cover price.

Stephen King and Dan Brown might be able to fly around the world on their private jets, but for many of the names you find in bookstores, writing is a second job. According to Morris Rosenthal, author of *Print-on-Demand Book Publishing: A New Approach to Printing and Marketing Books for Publishers and Self-Publishing Authors,* a book with a sales rank on Amazon of 5,000 will sell around 90 copies a week on the site. The company's sales of books, music, and DVDs totaled $5.35 billion in 2008, while Barnes & Noble and Borders together sold $8.35 billion worth of media. If every sale on Amazon represents another 2.5 sales in bookstore chains, then a book that makes it into top 5,000 of the world's biggest bookseller will be moving a total of around 900 copies a month.

If the book sells for $24.95 and the author's royalty is 15 percent, he or she would be taking home no more than $1,350 per month—a nice additional income but not something to give up the day job for. And your book has to be among the top 5,000 of Amazon's 4 million to earn it.

Of course, all of those are back-of-the-envelope calculations. Publishing is terribly complicated, and the figures can range all over the place, usually downward, but my experience is that they provide a pretty good guideline. When you've just seen an e-book generate $10,000 in two days, traditional publishing really doesn't look very tempting.

But print books can deliver two things that e-books can't. The first is distribution. Amazon might be the biggest bookseller in the world, and it is possible now to offer e-books and even your own Kindle books directly from the site, but it's still only one out-let. According to research company IbisWorld, the United States had around 34,000 bookstores as of 2008. Although the number is declining, that's still a massive market that an e-book can't reach.

The other benefit of a printed book is even more important. Being an established author gives you prestige.

Becoming a traditional author is difficult. You have to create a detailed proposal that explains what your book is about, describe the competition, and say how your book will be different. You have to send it to publishers and agents and hope that one of them is interested enough to bite. As the publisher of a popular web site, you'll have an advantage. Your site will give you a platform, a built-in audience that's already keen to learn about your book. But you'll still have to be prepared to absorb lots of rejection.

For publishers, every new book is like investing in a new business venture. They want to be as certain as they can be that the money they spend on the advance, on printing, and on marketing is going to come back. The safest response is always no.

This means that those authors who have made it through the process, whose names appear on the covers of books, and whose pictures can be found on shelves in stores have an unbeatable level of prestige. If a publishing company considers them expert enough to back with its money, then potential readers should trust them, too. Being able to say that you're a published *author,* in the traditional sense of the word, immediately puts you head and shoulders above your competitors. It delivers extra traffic to web sites, increases the sales of affiliate products you want to promote, leads other entrepreneurs to want to partner with you, and can even give you a path toward a career as a professional speaker.

So even though my AdSense book was doing very well without ever seeing the bottom of a printer tray, I wasn't completely against the idea of creating a traditional book.

What really got me interested was Morgan James's business model. Morgan James (www.MorganJamesPublishing.com) produces traditional books, but it doesn't act in a traditional way. Instead, it produces "entrepreneurial books," which bridge the gap between *traditional publishers* who produce books by taking all of the risk and in return giving authors a tiny share of the sales, and *vanity publishers* (aka self-publishers) who give authors all of the profits but also a giant financial risk (and none of the prestige).

As with self-publishing, you will have to reach into your pocket to publish with Morgan James. You'll have to pay for the design work, the editing, and the printing (although that also means you maintain control, whereas in traditional publishing, you don't even get the last word on the book title). That might cost you around $4,000, give or take. But unlike the self-publishing companies, Morgan James hasn't yet earned a penny. The company starts to make money only when your book starts to sell, so it won't give you a pile of books and leave you to it. Morgan James helps you to market the book as well. Most important, it does that by using the Ingram Book Group,

Figure 4.2   Morgan James will publish your book, put it in stores, and help you with the marketing.

a wholesaler and distributor—and the main channel for any book that wants to reach mainstream bookstores (Figure 4.2).

Produce your book with Morgan James, and you will be able to see it in your local bookstore.

There are other benefits, too. Because you've taken on more of the risk, you'll not only have more control, you'll also have higher rewards: Royalties at Morgan James are as high as 20 percent of the sales price, much higher than anything you can find in traditional publishing. And you get to keep the rights to your book.

That's very important. It means that you can put the same material on your web site, in e-books, and even turn it into a course if you want without receiving legal letters from a publishing company highlighting the clauses in the giant contract you signed that prohibit you from earning from your knowledge in any "unauthorized" way.

Morgan James, however, isn't open to everyone. The company receives about 4,500 manuscripts each year . . . and produces about 163. In terms of rejection, it's not too different from a traditional publishing company. But if you have a good idea, and if you're serious about creating and promoting the book, then it can deliver some huge benefits for entrepreneurial authors—business-minded people who want to help other business-minded people succeed.

The print book that I agreed to create with David Hancock went on to become a *New York Times* best-seller, giving me the kind of prestige and profile that I could never have earned any other way.

Morgan James can propel rising entrepreneurs to a whole new level. It's like giving your store a complete makeover, moving it up from a high-end shopping mall to a swanky Fifth Avenue boutique. You're still making money. You're still pushing buttons and hearing KaChings. But people look at you differently.

Morgan James is very selective and demands an investment from its authors. It's not right for everyone. There is an alternative, though. Printing technology has now evolved to a point where it's possible to produce a single copy of a book and still make the effort financially worthwhile. Some of the companies that do the printing are even plugged into the main book distribution systems, enabling you to create a book and put it on Amazon and even in stores without having to fill your garage with boxes of unsold books. Not only will you be able to sidestep the big publishing companies standing in the way of your printed book, you'll be able to become your own publishing company, producing your own books with practically no up-front costs at all.

I had the opportunity to interview David Hancock regarding the entrepreneurial publishing model. You can download the MP3 audio at www.MadeEasyPublishing.com.

You create the book and then promote it on your web site and through affiliate networks. But the book isn't printed until the order is received.

A number of companies offer services like this. Lulu (www.lulu.com) is perhaps the easiest and offers a wide range of different kinds of books, from publisher-grade soft-cover to case-wrapped hard-cover versions. The printing costs depend on the kind of book you want and the number of pages, but start at $5.30. Because you can set your own price, you're guaranteed to make a profit on every sale. Amazon has its own self-publishing arm at CreateSpace (www.createspace.com).

If you want to kick it up a bit, Lightning Source (www. lightningsource.com) works with some of the world's biggest publishing companies. You have to apply to join its program, so it's a bit selective, but this company is also plugged into Ingram's, so you'll have an easier time getting exposure, both in bookstores and online.

The advantages of print-on-demand should be clear: There's no risk, and you're in control. The disadvantage is that because it's not as selective as traditional publishing, it's also not as prestigious. It can, however, make a useful alternative to an e-book for buyers who prefer to hold their books in their hands (Figure 4.3).

Finally, when it comes to creating print books, there's always traditional publishing. Because traditional publishing is so selective, it's probably best to think of approaching major publishers as the last step on the ladder. You'll find it much easier to get agreement for your book idea if you can already show that people are buying your e-book or your print-on-demand book, if your blog has lots of readers, and if you already have a following. At that point, the publisher can see that your knowledge has value and that people are willing to pay for it. You represent a much lower risk.

Figure 4.3   Photopreneur (www. blogs.photopreneur.com), a blog that helps photography enthusiasts earn from their hobby, earns revenue with its print-on–demand photography book.

BECOME A STAR WITH DVDs AND WEBINARS

For many of the people looking to earn from their knowledge online, selling their expertise isn't new. In addition to setting up web sites that explain how to invest wisely, write computer programs, or build better gardens, they also teach courses. Those might be small private workshops, or they could be evening classes at a local adult education center. Certainly, when you can build an audience at a class like that, you can also build an audience online and earn from it.

Once your site is up and running, and once it has regular readers enjoying your knowledge, you should find that many of your readers will want individual, one-on-one learning opportunities. They don't just want to read the articles you're putting on your web site, they want to see you presenting that information in person. They want you to have the time to go into detail, and they want to be able to ask questions as you teach. When I asked my followers on Twitter what I should offer as a prize for a competition giveaway, the most requested item wasn't an iPhone, a new laptop, or even a lifetime's supply of pizza. It was a one-on-one lesson.

Again, this is something that works well across every subject. Just as you can pay for classes on everything from flower arranging to zoology, so you can create a visual information product based on your expertise and sell it online.

The easiest method is simply to record one of your classes. If you teach regularly, just put a video camera at the back of the room and let it run. You can always edit it later. If that approach is good enough for C-Span, it's good enough for you. If you don't teach regularly, just hold one class. Put on a seminar for people in your area and record it. Pack it with practical information, and you'll be able to burn it onto DVDs and sell it online as an information product. You'll make money once from the people who attend your seminar, and you'll continue making money from the DVDs that you sell.

There are plenty of DVD fulfillment companies around that will handle the copying and printing for you. Prices vary according to the design of the cover and the number of copies, but you can expect to pay no more than around $5 for each DVD. When LearningGuitarNow.com (www.learningguitarnow.com) can sell a six-DVD slide guitar course for $99, you should be able to pick up a big KaChing with every sale for discs of your classes.

Filming yourself teaching and putting the footage on DVD does mean selling a physical information product. That's very useful when you're giving talks or putting on demonstrations. But when you're selling online, of course, it's not necessary. You can also create webinars and make them viewable for a fee, using PayPal or E-junkie to allow access. There's plenty of software around, such as Glance (www.glance.net) and GoToWebinar (www.gotowebinar.com) that make the whole creation process very simple. The best way to learn how to use them is to do it. Try them out, practice, and you'll soon discover that creating webinars really doesn't demand any great skill at all.

The same principle holds true for webinars and information products: They have to contain solid, practical information. Watch other webinars to see how other people do it, then slot your expertise into their models.

One neat strategy is to use the information webinar not as a product itself, but as the free sample you use to sell a different information product. The post explaining the FTC rules that I put on my blog, for example, was very popular. But it was also light. The rules were horribly complex, and it's very easy for online sellers to make a mistake that could cost them dearly. So my lawyer, Kevin Houchin, got together with a bunch of other legal minds—people who specialize in contract and commercial law—and produced a 230-page toolkit that explained exactly how the new rules worked. Buyers also received modifiable legal documents and regular updates as the rules were applied in the real world.

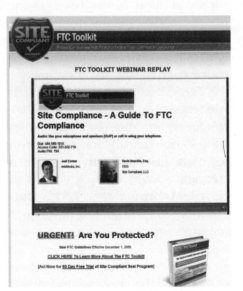

Figure 4.4   The Site Compliance webinar provided solid information and helped Kevin sell his FTC toolkit.

I know that a lot of work and expertise went into creating that information product, and I also know that the risks involved in not following the FTC's guidelines—even accidentally—could be massive. So at $97 for 230 pages of legal advice I was certain they'd need some pretty big servers to handle the demand.

Kevin's a good friend and I wanted to help him, so to bring in buyers, we put on a free one-hour webinar (Figure 4.4). You can see that webinar at www.sitecompliant.com/webinar.php. You'll see that first we used the webinar to capture e-mail addresses. Again, we don't sell those e-mail addresses. Kevin just uses them to send potential buyers information about the legal aspects of doing business online. If they don't want to receive that knowledge, they can unsubscribe. Kevin's challenge is to make the information he supplies so interesting that no one wants to unsubscribe and that people who didn't buy his FTC toolkit the first time they saw it do so in the future.

Users then receive a confirmation e-mail containing a link to the webinar itself. We tried to pack as much vital information as we could into that webinar, but we didn't think that people would want to watch for more than an hour. To discover the rest, they'd have to buy Kevin's kit, which is advertised at the bottom of the page.

So you can put your information on DVDs and sell them online like any other product. You can create a webinar and sell access to it. And you can use that webinar as a free sample of the information that you have available in your premium information product.

Is all of that stuff easy? Moderately. As with anything, when you know how, it's a breeze. Creating DVDs and producing webinars doesn't require any specialized knowledge. You just have to do it. The first time will be confusing. The second time will feel a little more comfortable. The third time you open the webinar software or upload your class footage to a DVD fulfillment company, you'll wonder why everyone isn't doing this.

ONLINE TRAINING PROGRAMS

A webinar is usually about an hour. That's not a lot of time, but it's enough to provide an introduction to a topic or go into detail about one strategy. A DVD course might consist of multiple discs and take several hours. An alternative approach is to create a complete online training course. Instead of being delivered on a disc, these classes can be taken on the Web. Once you've created the course, you'll be selling access—exactly like a webinar.

Creating a course isn't as difficult as it sounds. Software company Articulate (www.articulate.com), for example, has a range of e-learning programs. They're not cheap, but they do come with a free trial that lets you see that they really do create some attractive courses.

This isn't a product that's going to suit every publisher or every topic. But if your subject can be turned into a long-term course, and if your site has a large enough audience to generate sufficient sales, the $399 or so that Articulate's main course design program costs should start to look like a very good deal.

Books—both digital and traditional—DVDs, webinars, and online courses are just some of the ways that you can create information products. Online entrepreneurs are using these methods, and I have successfully used many of these methods, too. But it's not the format that's important. It's always the information.

Get that right and the format is just a way of delivering your expertise to your buyers—and hearing a KaChing.

Writing Copy that Sells

Once you've created your information product—whatever kind of product it is—the next step is to build a sales page that pitches it.

Of course, you'll already have a web site that has regular readers, trust, and brand value. You won't have to do more than mention that you have a book available for many of those users to rush out and give you your first KaChing. That's the result of the online sales process: Like me, know me, trust me, pay me.

Your regular readers will have already gone through the first three stages, so when you bring out your product, they'll be ready for the last stage.

But you don't want to market only to your regular readers. You also want to bring in readers of other web sites—anyone, in fact, who might have an interest in the information your product contains. You won't have time to lead those new people through that sales process. You'll want to convert them right away by persuading them, as soon as they reach your page, of the benefits of your product.

That means creating a page filled with effective sales copy—and usually that means creating a one-page sales letter.

You've probably seen these letters online before. They're unique to the Internet. Head to sales conferences and you'll be given brochures, flyers, and all sorts of different promotional material, but nothing comes close to the length, detail . . . and sheer persistent power of an online one-page sales letter.

That's because offline, space costs money. The more content that sellers want to put in their sales materials, the greater their printing costs. When you're printing thousands of copies at a time, those differences matter. On the Web, it doesn't matter how much text you place on a page. While packing a page with too many videos and images can slow loading time, you won't pay any more for space on the server—and that extra weight is unlikely to be a problem with a sales letter, anyway.

When you're selling online, you're free to go on and on . . . and on about all the benefits that your product can bring. Sales letters can be thousands of words long and offer testimonial after testimonial and subheading after subheading. They're enormous.

But they work. In one test conducted by *Marketing Experiments Journal* in 2004, long-form sales letters consistently outperformed short copy, sometimes by as much as 400 percent. In my own experience, I've seen upsells and one-time offers produce conversion rates as high as 70 percent. That doesn't always happen. In fact, it doesn't happen often, but I've never had it happen with any other sales technique.

The reason that well-written long-form sales letters work is that they accomplish two goals. First, they have the freedom to describe every sales point and answer every objection that can be raised from every reader. That's also why they're so long: they have a lot of work to do.

And the other reason they work is that their sheer bulk creates the impression that this product will do everything you could want and more. They bludgeon the reader into submission. One of the most common reactions to reading a one-page sales letter is, "Okay, I get it. How much is it already, and where's the buy button?" When you have readers asking that question, you should have no problem at all converting them.

Of course, the downside of a sales page that long is that no one actually reads it. Or rather, no one reads every word of a sales letter. But that's the beauty of one-page sales letters: They don't have to.

Different readers will have different objections and will be persuaded by different benefits. As readers scan a sales letter, the format of the page—the subheadings, the bolding, the italics, and the testimonial boxes—will help them to notice the points and arguments that are most likely to push *their* buttons. Readers will begin at the top and, as they scroll down the page, stop naturally at the areas that interest them the most. Those subheadings and boxes provide easy entry and exit points.

All of that information overload has another benefit: The details leave the reader more than satisfied. Whatever your product does, you're going to have competitors. Saturate your readers with information, and they're going to be less likely to look elsewhere for a similar product. If they don't buy from you, they're not going to want to start reading another sales letter all over again.

One-page sales letters that promote information products aren't subtle. They're not meant to be. But they are effective, and they need to be well written.

Usually, the best way to produce a sales letter is to hire an experienced copywriter to do it for you. Freelance services like eLance (www.elance.com) can be good places to look, and you can also try writing agencies like Scribat (www.scribat.com). Be sure to look at samples, but don't expect the writer to be able to provide conversion results. Clients rarely share them with the writers who produce their sales letters. You'll have to look at the sales letters and judge for yourself how persuasive they are.

It's also possible to write sales letters yourself. Although they look tricky, sales letters actually follow a very rigid structure and use all sorts of little copywriting tricks to lead readers to believe that they need your product. You'll start with a gripping headline that attracts attention, lays out the problem, indicates that you have the solution, and describes the benefits that those solutions will bring.

Subheadings are used to break up the sales letter and introduce new benefits, while testimonials help to build the trust you'll need to make the sale. You can get those testimonials by handing review copies of your product to friends and colleagues and asking them to say something nice if they like it. Just make sure that you follow the FTC's finicky new guidelines.

If you don't want write it from scratch, there are plenty of templates available that you can use to form your sales letter. My friend Michel Fortin, who has been called "the best sales-letter writer on the Internet," has created a very neat program called ScribeJuice that makes the whole process very simple. You can find it at www.scribejuice.com. Even if you prefer to hire a writer rather than try to do it yourself, check out the sales letter on that page; it's a perfect example of how a sales letter should work:

- The gripping headline provides a solution to a big problem right away.

- Bullet points at the first scroll down the page sell the benefits, not the features.

- The red subheadings create urgency.

- The black subheadings describe the content so that readers are able to spot the features that appeal to them.

- And there are tons of testimonials that deliver that trust.

Notice how Michel offers different products and uses an e-mail field to capture the addresses of people who haven't been persuaded. He's likely to pick up a very high conversion rate with a sales letter this good, but he's not going to turn everyone into a buyer. In addition to sales immediately, he'll also pick up plenty of near misses that he'll be able to convert in the future with mailings and bonuses.

One advantage of using a template system like Michel's is that you have the freedom to test different sales letters. That can be very helpful. You can even do this before you begin selling. Create three different kinds of sales letter and instead of collecting payments, invite readers to leave their e-mail addresses so that they can be contacted when the product is ready. Keep track of which sales letter brings in the most addresses, and by the time you're ready to launch you'll have a list of people you can pitch to directly—and you'll know which sales letter delivers the best conversions.

Recruiting Your Affiliate Sales Team

The sales letter acts as a kind of sales assistant. It talks to your leads, persuades them to buy, and takes their money. It goes KaChing. But you still have to bring those leads into your store. Your web site will act as one gateway; search engines will provide another. But you want more than that. You want to recruit other publishers in your field as sales assistants for your product.

You want to build up a team of affiliates.

Affiliate selling is one of the Internet's biggest success stories. I couldn't tell you how much money I've made as an affiliate, promoting other people's products on my web sites; it's always been one of my biggest and most reliable revenue streams. In Chapter 5, I explain how you can do the same thing. First, you should know how to recruit affiliates to sell your product for you.

The principle is very simple. Other people in your field will recommend your product to their users. In return for cashing in on the trust that they've built up, you have to give them a share of the sales price. That share can be pretty big. Half isn't unusual, and some sellers in very competitive fields have even been known to give away as much as 70 percent of their revenue to affiliate sellers.

The best way to calculate how much you should be giving away is to do the research. Search for other information products in your field and look at their affiliate programs. If you find that affiliate commissions for products similar to yours range from 35 to 50 percent, there's little point in trying to buy market share by offering more. In fact, doing that could even signal that you think your product can only attract affiliates based on sales volume. Affiliates want products that sell and that please their users. Those sorts of products can offer lower commissions. Amazon, for example, has one of the lowest payouts on the Web, with commissions for sellers as low as 4 percent. But it can get away with those low percentages because it has such a trusted brand that people are not hesitant to buy from Amazon.

To keep track of the amounts you need to pay your affiliates, they're assigned a unique code that's worked into the link that they use to send you traffic. A software program tracks that code automatically assigning the right commissions to the right referers.

It's a simple idea that's helped individuals and companies make millions online, both as publishers and as affiliates.

There are two ways to get your product into the hands of affiliate sellers.

The first is to build your own affiliate program. As always, there are a number of different software programs available that make the process relatively painless. (Once a system is shown to work on the Internet, you can be sure that it won't be long before some smart people bring out tools to make that system easy to use.) For example, iDevAffiliate (www.idevdirect.com) is just one program among many. It lets you hand out affiliate codes, track sales, and manage commissions.

These sorts of programs can be a little complex, but it's worth putting in the time to play with them and understand how they work—and how they can work for you. Consider it part of your online business training. Even if you decide to focus primarily on third-party affiliate agencies, it's still worth having your own affiliate system in place so that you can recruit sellers directly.

You might well find that it's those connections that bring in the biggest affiliate sales.

I constantly receive e-mails, tweets, and messages from people asking if I'd be willing to promote their product to my web site users. With their generous affiliate commission, they tell me, we're both guaranteed to make a fortune, so what do I have to lose?

The answer is *trust,* which is why I turn down just about all of those requests. I'm not going to recommend a product that I haven't tried or that I don't know. That doesn't mean that I never offer affiliate products to my lists. As you'll see in Chapter 5, I do that frequently and make good money from those offers. But they always come from people I know, people I trust, and usually people I've met at conferences. Because I know they deliver good information, I *want* to tell my readers about them. And because they know me, those publishers are prepared to tell their readers about my products—on an affiliate basis—in return.

In addition to creating your own affiliate management system, you should also be looking at using third-party agencies. You can think of these as giant wholesale warehouses in which producers pitch their wares to retailers. Those retailers can look at the details of the product, view how well they're selling and the commissions they offer, and decide whether to promote them themselves.

There are a bunch of different sites offering this service, but the market leader is ClickBank (www.clickbank.com). It costs $49.95 to join as a seller, but that can be recouped with just one or two sales, so the price shouldn't be an issue (Figure 4.5).

What will be an issue is the competition. Because ClickBank has such a massive collection of affiliate sellers and such a wide range of publishers, you're likely to find that your product is battling for eyeballs with lots of rivals—even if many of them are just plain poor.

ClickBank affiliates and buyers look for products that are growing in popularity, so to stand out on the site, it's important to generate sales from multiple affiliates. That will get your product rising up the ranks and attract attention. Use your own affiliate network, promote your product on your site and to your own

Figure 4.5 ClickBank brings your information product to cash registers across the Internet.

mailing list, and you'll find that success breeds success. The more sales you make on your own, the more affiliates you'll pick up on ClickBank—and the more sales those affiliates will generate for you.

There is one more thing that you can do to boost your affiliate sales: Encourage your sellers, especially your biggest sellers.

The 80/20 rule applies to affiliate networks as much as it does to every other part of your business: You'll find that most of your sales are coming from just a small section of your affiliate network. (It's likely that you'll also find that those super affiliates are the people you've recruited personally after meeting them at a workshop, seeing them at a conference, or communicating with them for a while online. They will often be people you know.)

Send all of your affiliates regular e-mails telling them about new product launches and suggesting the benefits of promoting your product. And send small gifts to your biggest affiliates to show how much you appreciate their work.

Add a Shopping Cart to Your Site

So you have a product. You have copy for your sales page, and you know how to recruit an army of sellers motivated to bring in a load of customers. You're almost ready to throw open the doors and hear your online cash registers KaChing out.

There's just one small problem.... You don't have any cash registers.

In order to sell your information product, you need a way for customers to choose the products they want and process a payment. As you might have guessed, that's all been systematized, simplified, and made a breeze. Just as you can now have a complete affiliate management program by doing little more than paying a few bucks for a piece of software, so is it possible to pay a company to handle the payment process for you.

Again, a number of different companies offer this service, but one of the best is E-junkie (www.e-junkie.com), which comes with all of the features that you'll find most useful, including buttons that you can just copy and paste, the ability to accept discount codes (allowing you to organize seasonal sales promotions), calculators

Figure 4.6   E-junkie (www.e-junkie.com) gives your
shoppers carts to load up on your goods.

for sales tax, VAT and shipping, and even an affiliate management
program (Figure 4.6).

For a fee that starts as low as $5 per month, you can upload
your product to E-junkie's servers. E-junkie will give you a button
that you can paste onto your site and your sales page. When buyers
click the button, they're taken through the payment process, using
PayPal, Google Checkout, and a bunch of other systems. Once the
payment has been made, E-junkie then directs customers to a download page. It can even handle physical goods such as books, CDs, and
DVDs.

In terms of technical demands, you won't need to know much
more than how to do Control-C (copy) and Control-V (paste) on
your keyboard in order to start making money.

The Big Launch!

Creating an information product takes time and effort. The process
of creating the product can take several months if it's a full-length
book—or even just a 100-page e-book. Writing the sales copy can
take time and money, and you still have to design and publish the
sales page and start building your network of affiliates.

At some point though, you'll be ready to start selling.

Now you could start slowly: Make the product available, put up a link on your web site, and start directing your readers toward your sales page. You'll hear a quiet but steady tinkle of KaChings. But that would be a waste of a valuable opportunity.

A launch is a tool that you can use to generate publicity, provoke word-of-mouth recommendations, and build the kind of buzz that brings even more sales. It's your product's birthday, a time to celebrate, throw open the doors, and get those cash registers ringing.

The preparation for a launch begins a long time before the launch itself. Most of that work will take place behind the scenes, but when you leak small snippets of what you're up to, you can help to build anticipation so that buyers are ready for your big announcement. You don't just want people to be interested in what you have to offer when you launch; you want them lining up with their wallets out.

For example, in November 2009, I launched a new online TV show. Obviously, my production team and I had put a huge amount of effort into creating the content, filming the action, and editing the footage. In order to prepare people for the show and to make sure that we were starting with an audience, we created a short teaser that we put on YouTube. I then posted a series of tweets that built interest.

The first tweet, posted on October 25, said simply:

"Saw finished edit of the NEW Joel Comm Show, to debut in mid-November. You are going to love it!"

Note that there was no link there and no further information. I wanted my followers on Twitter to ask questions. By holding information back, I built their curiosity.

Five days later, I went some way toward satisfying that curiosity by posting this tweet:

"It's the World Premier of the teaser for the NEW Joel Comm Show! ->http://TwitPWR.com/jcshow/- enjoy and plz RT! #joelcomm"

I followed that tweet up a few hours later with this one:

*"Would love to hear more comments on the teaser video for the NEW Joel Comm Show ->*http://youtube.com/joelcomm *- Premiers in November!"*

As of this writing, we're still at least two weeks away from the first show and at the moment, my followers can't do anything. They certainly can't watch anything, and I'm not selling anything. But I've already told them that something is coming, I've shown them a neat one-minute teaser, and by asking for their opinion, I have them talking about it. The excitement is building so that when we launch, people will be ready.

This kind of preparation is vital for getting the most out of launch day. It gives you the time to guide leads through that four-step sales process that ends with "pay me." It means that in the weeks before your product is available, your market will already be familiar with you. They'll have checked out your web site, followed you on Twitter, and joined your Facebook fan page. They'll already be willing to trust you, and they'll want to be a part of your success—and enjoy success themselves—by buying your new product.

And that preparation can make money, too. When Darren Rowse of ProBlogger used Twitter and his weekly newsletters to generate interest in his new photography e-book, he received both valuable feedback and orders for 50 copies, enough to cover his expenses.

The launch day itself becomes an opportunity, not to convert those leads (they should already have been converted; you'll just be giving them a way to spend their money), but to bring in new leads. Some of those leads will be converted right away by the persuasive power of your sales letter. Others will start going through that four-step sales process and buy from you in the future.

The main job of launch day is to attract attention, and there are lots of different ways to do that. Giveaways always work well. The best example occurred in July 2009 when Moonfruit, a web site development company that's part of SiteMaker, wanted to celebrate its tenth year in business: It chose to give away one MacBook Pro every day for 10 days. To enter the running, all Twitter users had to do was post a tweet with the hashtag "#moonfruit." Twitterers could post as many tweets as they wanted, with each tweet increasing the chances that they'd be selected. (Third-party applications like Twiveaway and Tweetaways automate the process of selecting a random giveaway winner and even notify them for you.)

The tweets came in at a rate of 300 posts per minute. Messages containing the hashtag were taking up almost 3 percent of Twitter's entire communications. For days, #moonfruit was the most popular trending term—and might have remained so if it hadn't mysteriously disappeared from the list of trending topics. Moonfruit's web site traffic increased by a factor of eight and sign-ups went up 100 percent.

That wasn't a launch (although you could call it a relaunch), and the idea wasn't completely original. Squarespace, a rival web site builder, had already tried something similar but fluffed it. Promising to give away 30 iPhones in 30 days, Squarespace instead handed out gift tokens. Moonfruit did better simply by delivering what it promised. The principle remains: A company picked up a huge amount of viral marketing and positive publicity to mark a special occasion. It did so by giving away something valuable.

If you decide to use a giveaway as a method of attracting eyeballs, the temptation will always be to give away copies of your own product. You'll be able to control delivery, and the costs will be minimal. There's nothing wrong with doing that, and I do it often. But giveaways of your own product appeal mostly to people who already know you and already know that they want your information. It excites your main market, but it can leave people who don't know you cold. Because they don't yet understand the value your information will bring them, they're not certain that they want to invest the time required to enter your giveaway and read your book.

Give away something that *everyone* wants, and you'll attract attention beyond your core audience. Gadgets, especially Apple products, always seem to do well, and I've picked up plenty of responses by offering a Flip Mino video recorder. Passing out products that are related to the subject of your information product whenever possible is also a good idea. That will get your promotion discussed among people who might not know you but are interested in your subject.

One of the criticisms of Moonfruit's campaign was that although it attracted attention to the company, it wasn't quite clear how many of those new users were interested in actually building a web site. As an advertising campaign, it was powerful but inaccurate. When a publisher supports an information product about tiling your own roof or earning money with pet photography by offering a free roofing hammer or a year's subscription to a photo hosting company, that giveaway is much more targeted.

Giveaways like these benefit your audience, but you can also add sparkle to your launch by giving things away to others. I once organized a tweetathon to mark a product launch, spending a day streaming live from my office as I chatted with other marketers and special guests. We raised a fair amount of money for WaterIsLife, had a great time, and also attracted quite a bit of media attention. The press love writing about businesses working for charities, because it makes them feel that they're helping charities, too. And audiences like taking part in charity events because it's such an easy way for them to give back.

Best of all, you actually do get to give back. A successful product launch makes you feel good, but actually *doing* good makes you feel so much better.

Finally, the preparation for just about every product launch will usually involve a press release. It's as traditional as tinsel on the Christmas tree and, too often, about as useful. The problem isn't that publicity isn't a valuable part of a product launch. In fact, it's an *essential* part of a product launch. It's that too few people understand how a press release works and how to use it.

Reporters aren't interested in telling the world that you have a new product. That's what their publication's advertising space is for. They're interested in telling their audience about things that are going to affect their lives.

When you come to write your press release, don't announce the launch of your new book or your new DVD course. Instead, write a press release that announces the changes that your new release will cause. If you'd created an information product that explains how to telecommute, for example, then your press release would sell the idea that no one need sit in rush hour traffic ever again. That would be the hook that would bring the reporters in. Quotes

> Reporter on deadline seeking input
> from educators about how-to of
> optimizing school district technology on
> a budget. DM me with contact info
> 6:35 PM Nov 13th from HootSuite   Reply Retweet
>
> **rjmcgarvey**
> Robert McGarvey

Figure 4.7 Freelance writer Robert McGarvey looks for help on Twitter—and hands out an offer of free publicity to companies with the knowledge he needs.

from the author of a new book, e-book, or course on telecommuting would prove what the reporter is saying—and give your product the publicity it needs.

Press releases like these are certainly useful, and you should be looking to shoot out a batch of them to support your release. But they aren't the only way to get publicity, and you shouldn't rely on them. There are also lots of reporters on Twitter who are looking for stories and sources, and connections with them can also be valuable routes to a newspaper's pages or even a television station's airtime (Figure 4.7).

The key here is not to pitch to them directly. No one likes being pitched to on Twitter, and waving at reporters in public is likely to turn them away. Instead, in the weeks leading up to the launch, add journalists to the lists of people you're following on the site. Listorious (www.listorious.com) will help you to find them; you can see lists of reporters broken down by region and even by newspaper. Join their conversations and be sure to answer any questions they might have. Reporters on Twitter also occasionally ask for help with sources, giving you easy interview opportunities and a chance to build a lasting contact. Make sure that you lend a hand whenever you can.

The real secret to winning tons of free publicity is very simple: Be successful.

Reporters are rarely the first to notice when something happens. They only notice the behavior of people who have already spotted it. My iFart app, for example, didn't cause a ripple in the press when it first came out. It was only after it had sold thousands of downloads and reached the top of the app charts that the press began paying attention.

When you want to attract the media's attention, try waving at your market.

All of these things will help to prepare your market even before your product becomes available. It ensures that potential customers already know you, like you, and trust you, and that they're ready to pay you as soon as you launch. On launch day—and in the days immediately following—you want to be ready to convert as many of those leads as possible.

Perhaps the most effective strategy to generate those sales is a time-limited offer. Again, Darren Rowse has shown just how effective that can be. In late 2009, his Digital Photography School site launched an e-book about portrait photography. Although Darren is a hugely experienced blogger whose sites give him a very handsome income and the author of a book about professional blogging, this was the first time that his Digital Photography School had launched a product. In a blog post on his site, ProBlogger.net, Darren explained that his launch strategy consisted of the following:

- An e-mail to his newsletter list

- A post on his Digital Photography School web site

- Promotions to members of his forums

- Further mentions on Twitter to supplement the tweets he'd already posted

- A message to his community on Facebook

- Promoting through affiliates using E-junkie's affiliate service

- Asking friends and members of his network to give his book a mention and a link

Within 12 hours, he'd sold 950 copies. The e-book cost $19.95, but for the first nine days, customers could buy it at a 25 percent discount. By the time the nine-day launch period had ended and the e-book was available at full price, he'd sold 4,800 copies, grossing a total of almost $72,000. Not all of that was profit, of course. PayPal's fees meant that actual revenues were slightly smaller, and there were production costs to pay for the e-book's design, proofreading, and commissioned content. Affiliates also took their cut. But there's still no doubt those nine days were extremely profitable, helped by an offer that came with a clear deadline. And it's the deadline that's important, not the price. Sales continued to come in at the same rate even after the price went up, pushed by the momentum created by the launch. The deadline pushed leads to buy immediately instead of putting the decision off till later—or never.

Those nine days might have been more profitable, though. The graph showing sales of the e-book over the nine-day launch period looked like a V. More than 1,000 copies were sold on the official launch day, creating an immediate spike. Sales then declined before spiking again at the end of the launch period, when Darren sent out a second e-mail reminding readers that they had only 36 hours remaining to buy the book at a 25 percent discount. That e-mail generated almost 1,200 sales.

Other marketers have pointed out that that's a fairly typical pattern, but it can be improved. Jeff Walker, for example, did a midlaunch promotion, turning the V shape into a W shape by adding some additional bonuses halfway through the launch period. Leads who had seen the first e-mail and decided to think about it were converted then, and fewer were lost before the end of the campaign.

Darren also felt that he could have put more work into encouraging his affiliates. Only two or three, he said, generated significant sales. That's an easy mistake to make, especially for people with experience of earning as an affiliate. It's easy to forget that not everyone understands the importance of recommending the product, talking about it, and making the affiliate link both unobtrusive and easy to find. It pays to make affiliate work part of the preparation by ensuring a good choice of banners for publishers to use, keeping them informed about the launch campaign, explaining what they can do to increase sales—and recruiting as many as possible.

It's a lot of work, but when the rewards are almost $8,000 a day, it's worth putting in the effort.

That's the story of information products. They're another way to transmit the information that you have about your passion or your profession to people who want to learn that knowledge—and get paid for it. The products themselves can come in a range of sizes and formats; they can be sold online using a team of affiliates and delivered using an automated shopping cart system that's a breeze to add to your site.

They take effort. While you can be up and earning with a web site in days, a good information product may well take weeks to put together, as well as the time and expense to create an optimal sales page promoted by a cadre of affiliates.

But once that's finished, you'll be able to relax. The money will come in by itself, in a constant stream and entirely automated. You'll be able to kick back and enjoy the chime of the KaChings.

Earning from Affiliate Programs

In Chapter 4, I talked about selling your knowledge to others in the form of an information product, and I pointed out that a vital part of the marketing process is creating a network of affiliates to do the pushing for you.

Those affiliates aren't promoting your product just because they like you. They *should* like you—and they certainly won't help you if they don't like you—but that's not the reason they're selling your goods. They're promoting your product because you're paying them. You're giving them a share of the sales price, turning them into sales reps working entirely on commission. Clearly, should those affiliates find that they're not making money out of the deal, they're going to be doing something else. The fact that affiliates continue to promote your goods shows that they're winning.

If those affiliates can make money from selling products on a commission basis, so can you.

This isn't a case of either/or. You don't have to choose between making money as an affiliate and making money by creating products for affiliates. I create and market information products, selling them through affiliate networks. I'm also an affiliate, selling products created by other producers. In fact, my sites generate five-figure monthly incomes from affiliate sales alone. As always, when you're looking to make your Internet business KaChing, you want it to KaChing in all sorts of different ways.

Earning as an affiliate is different from the revenue strategies we've seen so far. When you make money from the ads on your web site, you're trading on your expertise. Users will come to your site to pick up your free knowledge. Put the smartly targeted ads that companies like Google and Chitika supply in all of the right places and you'll earn money as users click through to other sites offering information on the same topic.

When you create an information product, you'll be selling your knowledge directly. The format is just a way of transmitting that knowledge. The sales page, sales network, shopping cart, and launch publicity are just the technicalities. They're the methods you use to deliver as many copies as possible to as many people as possible—and earn as much money as possible. Just as it's the quality of the information you supply in your content that will determine how popular your site becomes, so it's the quality of expertise in your information product that will influence how many downloads you achieve.

When you sell as an affiliate, the quality of the information is still important. But you don't get to change it; you only get to choose it. If the product you're thinking about promoting doesn't contain knowledge good enough to help your users, then you should give it a pass. The amount you'll earn as an affiliate won't depend on the quality of *your* knowledge but on the quality of the *seller's* knowledge.

What you bring to the party is trust.

Your web site will give you an audience. As they're enjoying your content, you're going to bother them by letting them know about a product that they didn't know they needed and have probably never heard of. They may buy it, if *you* tell them they should.

The product could cost $97, $199, or even more. If your audience saw it in a store, they would probably walk on by. But because *you've* told them that this is a product they need to own, many of them will click the link, press the shopping cart button, and make a purchase, thus putting money in your pocket.

That's the power of a good web site, packed with reliable, quality content. That's the power that the trust of your users can bring.

In this chapter, I explain how to make money as an affiliate. I start with a brief description of what being an affiliate means, then discuss how to find merchants and how to sign up for their programs. Finally, I share details of the strategies for success that allow me to enjoy a deafening level of KaChing from the affiliate ads I place on my web sites and deliver to my e-mail subscribers.

So, What Exactly Is an Affiliate?

Publishers call themselves *affiliates,* Amazon calls them *associates,* and people more used to selling in the offline world tend to use a simpler term: *sales rep.*

The offline term is wrong. Amazon's term is wrong, too, even though the company was one of the first to offer an affiliate program back in 1996. Affiliate systems have developed a lot since then.

An affiliate isn't quite a sales rep. Sales reps have no say in the products they sell. Their companies give them a suitcase full of samples and tell them they can keep a share of whatever they earn. They are *employees* . . . even if their income depends entirely on their sales skills.

Affiliates are really *entrepreneurs.* They choose which products they sell, they build their own markets, and they decide on the best way to persuade people to buy. They also don't rely on those sales to make money from the market.

That affiliates are independent business owners in their own right is important. It means that sellers have to treat them with respect—and pay them far more than they might be willing to pay an employee. And it also means that affiliates have to take responsibility. Your earnings as an affiliate will depend to a large extent on the quality of the product you're selling, but they will also depend on your connection with your market and your ability to lead your readers to buy.

The concept behind affiliate selling is very, very simple. You choose a product, present it to your market, and you take a share of the sales price when one of your users buys. (Although you might find a few affiliate sellers offering payments on a cost-per-action or even cost-per-click basis, around 80 percent of affiliate systems are believed to operate according to cost-per-sale basis, the model whereby you earn a commission.)

Making a lot of money out of affiliate selling requires a little skill. That starts with finding the right merchants to work with.

Choosing Merchants that Match Your Market

Office Depot, Gap, Target, Toys "R" Us, Amazon.com, Zappos .com ... if you can name a big retailer selling online, in the real world, or both, you'll find that they have an affiliate program that lets anyone help move their inventory.

Why shouldn't they have an affiliate program? There's no risk—they only have to pay if someone actually makes a sale—and if they don't offer an affiliate program, a publisher working in the field will put a competitor's ads on that site instead. Retailers that don't have affiliate programs risk losing market share.

That means you're spoiled with choices. But it also means that many of those choices will be bad. Some products will always sell better to your market than others, and some sellers will suit you and your users better than others.

The first challenge you'll have as an affiliate seller is trying to predict which items you should be recommending to your audience—and from which sellers.

In theory, that's not as difficult as it sounds ... and yet so many people get it wrong. In a survey of 450 affiliates conducted in 2009 by AffStat.com, part of affiliate guru Shawn Collins's Affiliate Summit, 23 percent of respondents said that they chose affiliate merchants based on their management systems. A similar number made their decision based on brand awareness, and almost a quarter made it based on the company's payout level.

Only 3 percent chose a merchant based on its relevance to their web site. That might explain why almost half of those affiliates were earning less than $500 a month. However, 4 percent were making between $10,000 and $20,000 a month, and 17 percent said that they were making more than $20,000 every month. If you get your affiliate system right, you really can make your business KaChing! But you have to get it right.

That starts with choosing your merchants.

You really have a choice of two different routes. Affiliate networks like Commission Junction and ClickBank act as clearinghouses for merchants. You can browse around, look for a product that suits your content, and add it to your site.

This approach works best when you have lots of sites on lots of different topics and are hoping that affiliate revenues will give you a little extra each month. From the publisher's point of view, the process couldn't be simpler: Sign up, pick a product, and place the ad on your page. Whatever sales you earn will be a nice little bonus and could mount up when placed across a large network of different sites.

The alternative is to take the ads directly, either from a trusted retailer or from the producer. I've already explained how you can create your own affiliate network to promote your product, but not all producers do this, especially when their products are physical. While creators of handcrafted wooden toys might be fine about shipping off their goods to occasional buyers brought in by affiliates, large producers usually prefer to send their products in bulk to a wholesaler or to large retailers. They then rely on those businesses to bring in the buyers.

If you want to sell an information product, it's likely that you'll be able to join the producer's own affiliate program. If you want to offer the kind of product you can find in stores, you'll probably be looking at the affiliate programs of major retailers—giving you a bit of a headache as you try to weigh up the benefits of each.

Whichever approach you take—whether you're looking at an affiliate network or the programs of different retailers—you'll find there are lots of different criteria that you can use to judge their programs. Different affiliate merchants will offer different sales percentages, have different kinds of ads, provide different minimum payout levels, and offer customer service of variable quality.

All of those things are important. But none of them are as important as whether your customers trust the merchant enough to buy.

With a maximum commission of just 15 percent, Amazon has one of the lowest-paying affiliate systems (Figure 5.1). Yet its

Figure 5.1 Amazon's Associates program lets you offer any of the company's products in a huge range of different ways ... for a commission of up to 15 percent. In practice, the commission is usually much lower.

program is also one of the most popular, partly because it offers a huge range of products, but mostly because people trust the company. If they've bought from Amazon before, they understand how it works, and they know that it won't pocket their credit card details for nefarious purposes.

Put an affiliate ad from Amazon on your site, and the trustworthiness of the merchant isn't an issue. The only remaining challenge will be whether you can persuade your users that the product is worth buying.

You can spend a huge amount of time browsing affiliate networks in your search for the perfect merchant for your site. You can lose hours comparing commission rates, reading reviews from other sellers, and trying to second-guess the kind of service you'll get from the merchant's affiliate manager. But when you're using affiliate products as an additional sales channel to complement your other methods of generating a KaChing, the most important factor will be the ease with which you can move users from browsers to buyers. You want to make sure that there are as few obstacles as possible on the way to the cash desk. That means choosing a merchant you believe will be familiar to your users and one with whom they're used to doing business.

Usually, that's pretty clear. If you want to promote a book on a topic related to the subject of your article, then it's likely that Amazon will be the most trusted retailer. Things get a little more complex when you have a real choice between similar outlets offering competing affiliate programs. Photographers, for example, can now earn a little money by submitting their images to microstock sites, which license them to publishers in return for a fee. Each of those sites has an affiliate program that reflects the sorts of users it needs most. iStockphoto (www.istockphoto.com), the most popular microstock site, pays a one-time $10 bounty for new customers and nothing for new photographers. BigStockPhoto (www.bigstockphoto.com) pays $5 for new photographers and 35 percent of the value of the first sale for new buyers. Dreamstime (www.dreamstime.com) has the potential to be the most lucrative of all: It pays affiliates 10 percent of what referred photographers earn and what referred buyers spend for up to three years.

It might seem that Dreamstime's affiliate program offers the best deal. But if photographers don't feel that Dreamstime will sell their photos, then they won't sign up. And if buyers don't feel that Dreamstime offers them a wide enough selection of pictures, then they won't buy any.

When that happens, affiliates earn 10 percent of nothing.

Similarly, a site with content aimed at photographers, but has very few images for buyers wouldn't make much money promoting iStockphoto, which pays nothing for new photographers.

These sorts of choices turn up across different fields. Amazon's Associate program is very different from that offered by Borders or the one offered by Barnes & Noble. While Borders pays according to a performance scale that tops out at 8.5 percent, Barnes & Noble pays a flat 6 percent. Amazon, with its front-page 15 percent boast, actually makes the choices even more complicated by offering two different kinds of affiliate programs: The company's Performance Fee structure has a scale that starts at 4 percent, and although it can reach 15 percent for *some* goods, it's unlikely that many "associates" would see those returns; the Classic Fee structure pays a flat 4 percent, significantly less than the affiliate would have earned for the same sale had he or she signed up with Barnes & Noble.

However, as a Barnes & Noble affiliate, that person might struggle to make the sale. Affiliates earn a commission only for online sales, and those are more likely to come from Amazon.

While it's easy to compare the details of different programs, without knowing the click-through rates of different programs and which kinds of audiences generated them, it's always very difficult to say which program would suit your site best.

Fortunately, there are a couple of ways to stumble toward the best option for your site. The first is to test out different programs. That will take awhile, but it's the only way to know for sure which program delivers the best results in practice.

The second way is to benefit from the experience of other publishers in your field. Lee Torrens, for example, is a microstock photographer whose blog Microstock Diaries (www.microstockdiaries.com) offers advice for other photographers looking to increase their picture sales. He also provides reviews and overviews of the site's affiliate programs so that photographers with web sites can add to their earnings through referrals as well as image sales. His site has become a major resource for photographers hoping to earn a little cash—and it helps them choose the right affiliate programs for their site, shortening their testing times.

You should find that this sort of information is available in many fields, and if it isn't available in yours, you know what to write your next blog about.

Choosing the Products that People Want

If assessing merchants and comparing programs can be a bit of a head-scratcher, choosing products should be a breeze.

The rule is: Choose products you know.

We've already seen how vital trust is in a successful affiliate program. When you feel confident that your users will get some real benefits out of using the product, they'll pick up on your enthusiasm. They'll also understand that every time you're offering a product for sale, you're not just doing it because you want to make a buck. They'll believe that you're doing it because you love using the product and that they'll love using the product, too.

This is one of the great things about adding affiliate links to a web site. Not only do you get to reward the creator of a product you like, you get to bring some real benefits to your users—and make money out of it, too. Perhaps the best place to look for products to recommend then is on your shelf and on your desk.

If you've bought something and enjoyed using it, then recommending it to the readers of your web site should be a breeze.

As with any rule, this one tends to be broken.

There are plenty of web sites making good money with affiliate links that lead to products the publisher has never heard of. My site DealofDay.com has plenty of affiliate links leading to products I've never tried. But the site isn't personal, and the range of goods on offer makes it clear that these links aren't recommendations. The site is offering opportunities, and the users are free to decide whether they want to make the most of them (Figure 5.2).

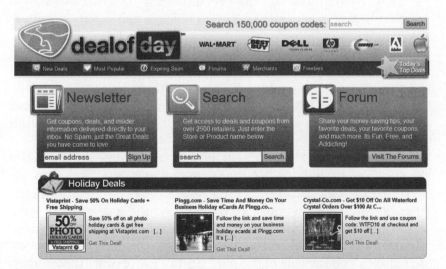

Figure 5.2   My DealofDay.com web site offers deals from thousands of retailers. These deals don't come recommended, but they do give shoppers a chance to pick up bargains—and this gives my site plenty of opportunity to earn affiliate income.

That creates a whole new kind of opportunity for publishers. If you write about products, however broad the range, you can still make money from affiliate links. The strategy here is mass marketing rather than niche marketing. Instead of promoting one carefully chosen product to people you know will like it, you offer lots of different products to a wide range of people and hope that there's enough variety to please everyone—or at least enough to give you a decent number of sales.

Sites like these aren't easy to create. They're also difficult to market. When you have a broad selection of products, all you can do is make them available. You can't push them directly to buyers, because no one will believe that you've used every product you're promoting. Even review sites, a useful way to add lots of affiliate products to a web site, can struggle a little here. If you write a negative review, no one will want to buy the product. You'll have killed your own commissions. But if you only write positive reviews, you'll kill the credibility of your site, something that's even more serious.

That doesn't mean you can't do it. Review sites that focus on a specific niche can generate very good revenue and supply plenty of opportunity to offer both helpful content and profit-generating ads.

AppCraver (www.appcraver.com), for example, is a site that provides short reviews of iPhone apps. The reviews each come with an affiliate link that leads to Apple's iTunes store, where readers can make a purchase. (Apple pays 5 percent commission for each sale.) But that's not the only way the site monetizes those reviews.

In fact, it's likely that most readers will decide to purchase directly from their iPhones rather than downloading first to iTunes and then moving the app to their mobile devices. So AppCraver offers an alternative way to turn users into cash. In addition to linking to apps, the site also runs a store that sells iPhone accessories. That store is operated as a separate site, but ads for specific products also run on the side of the page next to the reviews themselves (Figure 5.3).

When it comes to choosing products, you should find that being selective and recommending items you've used and loved should deliver high returns. It is also possible to build a site, such as a review

Figure 5.3 AppCraver provides reviews of iPhone apps, giving it plenty of opportunity to put up affiliate ads. One appears at the top of every review, while other graphic ads line the right side of the page. The left side leads to accessories available from the site's affiliate store.

site, that offers affiliate links to lots of different affiliate products. Just don't depend on those affiliate links alone to deliver all the KaChing the site can bring.

Strategies for Affiliate Success

When you're earning money with CPC ads, the strategy is simple. Write good content that attracts readers. Put up ads that match your content. Place those ads in prominent positions, and optimize them so that they look like content. Bring in the traffic, stand back and wait, and you should find that the KaChing starts to happen all by itself.

It's an amazing thing.

Earn on a CPM basis, and the strategy is even easier. Just bring in lots of users. Focus your efforts on traffic generation, and those CPM ads will add a little extra to your monthly income with no more effort.

When you're looking to add affiliate income to that revenue, though, the strategy is a little more complex. Success relies on the following factors.

THE RIGHT CHOICE OF PRODUCT AND MERCHANT

We've already seen how important this is. The merchant has to be trustworthy if the journey from page to cash desk will be smooth and obstacle-free. Top merchants understand that their trustworthiness has a value, and they often cash in on it by paying lower affiliate rates. If you feel that your users would think twice before buying from a merchant they're not familiar with, then it's worthwhile taking a little less from each sale but earning more through a greater overall sales volume.

When it comes to choosing the product, the safest bet is always to promote items that you know and believe in. You'll be able to offer them to your readers and feel that you're delivering something valuable. That's priceless.

Alternatively, you can offer a class of products, such as iPhone apps, gardening tools, or computer games. Create a web site that allows you to talk about lots of different models within that class, and you'll be able to use the affiliate ads as high-paying alternatives and additions to your CPC ads. That can be a useful strategy, too, especially for review sites.

Of course, whichever of those two strategies you follow, the products you offer must suit your audience. There's little point in showing an affiliate ad for a high-priced, high-commission product to people who aren't interested in buying it.

MAKE RECOMMENDATIONS

Sites that rely heavily on affiliate links, such as review sites, tend to be hard to build. They have to be planned deliberately: You have to know which products you want to write about, how you're going to write about them, and where you're going to source the affiliate links from. Usually, you'll want to make things as easy as possible by using as few merchants as possible. That will make the implementation easier, the stat-tracking clearer, and it's also likely to give you higher commissions as you sell more products for your merchant.

Placing occasional affiliate links to products you've used is always going to be easier. You won't need to create a dedicated web site, and you won't have to struggle to create reviews of products you haven't tried.

Whenever you use a product that you know your readers would like to use, you can write about it on your web site. You don't even have to create a dedicated blog post. Just mentioning it in a post you were going to write anyway can still generate sales.

In fact, that sort of casual approach often looks more natural, conferring even greater trust.

You can make this a regular event. If you find, for instance, that every time you recommend a product, you earn around $500 in commissions, then you can make that $500 a regular part of your income by making sure that you include a similar recommendation once a month. You wouldn't want to do it too often, because your conversion rate for each recommendation would fall—users will always have a limited budget—but every few weeks should be enough to give your income some reliable additional revenue.

It's the *recommendation* that's key here.

Affiliate advertising is unusual in that advertisers don't mind if you actively promote their products to your users. In fact, because they only have to pay you if your users actually give them money, they'll *want* you to push their products. The large merchants even have dedicated affiliate managers whose job includes offering tips to help with promotions. When a monetization system gives you that much independence and that much influence, it's a shame not to use it.

In general, the more intensely you recommend an affiliate product, the greater you can expect your conversion rate to be.

Those recommendations can come in all sorts of different forms. The most effective is always to say, "I've used this product, and it worked wonders. You should use it, too."

When you use this approach, bring it to life. Explain what brought you to the product, describe what it does, and point out several features that have really impressed you.

Here's an example of a short post for a recommended affiliate product—and a model—that you can use on your own web site:

Now I Know Where I Am

I always try to be punctual. I calculate how long it will take me to reach a destination. I leave with plenty of time for traffic jams. And I'm not afraid to stop doing whatever I'm doing—even when I'm in the flow—to make sure that I'm not late.

But I also have absolutely no sense of direction. It doesn't matter how many times I check the map, I'm practically guaranteed to make at least one wrong turn. Last week, for example, I had to take a parcel to the post office. (My sister just had a baby and B. wants to send her one of her quilts.) I must have been there a hundred times since we moved here but, sure enough, I took a wrong turn and ended up on the highway heading in the wrong direction.

I'd like to tell people that I'm always at least 10 minutes late because my life is so busy, but the truth is that it's because I never know where I am.

Last week, I finally gave in. I admitted that I'm hopeless and bought a GPS system. It's great. I went for the Magellan RoadMate 1470. So far, it's working great. The graphics are much easier to read than I expected them to be. The voice is clear and far less annoying than listening to the kids say, "Are we there yet?" And it hasn't once directed me into a river.

If you're geographically challenged like me, then you should get one. You might be able to finally get places on time.

There are a few points that you want to note before creating an affiliate-supported post like this. First, it's personal. It's filled with all sorts of little pieces of information that say something about the writer. The article doesn't just say the writer went to the post office, for example. It also says why he went and what was in the parcel. That brings the reader into his life and builds a personal connection. This isn't an ad; it's a friend telling another friend what he's been up to lately.

That's the kind of communication that leads to sales.

That's also why the post is lighthearted. It doesn't list all of the product's features, and it doesn't even say it's the best GPS system on the market. A review might do that, but when you're recommending a product that's worked for you, you won't know whether it's the best or just good enough.

All you can do is talk from your own experience, and your experience is that it was good enough for you. That's your advantage, and it's something that a post like this makes the most of.

If you're going to use this post as a model for regular, additional affiliate income on your web site, start by building context. Explain what led you to make the purchase so that the product's solution to your problem is clear. Make a few positive comments about the product. Don't go overboard (unless you really do believe that it's the greatest thing since the spam blocker). Just say what *you* like about the product the most.

Finally, end by suggesting that people who are like you—and that should be most of your readers—go out and buy one, too.

It's an approach that's subtle, easy to do, and doesn't make your users feel as though they're getting a hard sell. It won't turn you into an overnight millionaire, but it should deliver conversion rates of perhaps 1 to 2 percent.

That might not sound like much—it means that 99 out of every 100 readers aren't buying—but a product such as a GPS system costs about $135. On Amazon, that would mean an affiliate commission of around $5.40 for every sale. To earn $540 extra each month, you'd need make 100 sales during the month. At a modest 1 percent conversion rate, you'd need 10,000 unique users every month.

When you're generating that kind of traffic—and a site that's been up for a while *should* be generating that kind of traffic—that's the sort of boost to your income you can expect from just one short post recommending an affiliate product.

You can characterize a post like this as an "experience" recommendation. It's saying, "I've used this product. I like it. You're going to like it, too." You won't always be able to say that about every product you're going to offer because you won't be able to try every product. (Although, if you are managing to earn $500 a month through occasional affiliate recommendations, then spending $130 or so on a gadget that you can recommend is still going to look like a good deal. You'll be making a profit of $370 and have a cool new toy every month.)

An alternative approach is to recommend the producer.

This is something I do frequently. I know that if Yanik Silver or Shawn Collins or any of the other marketers I've met at conferences is bringing out a new product, it's going to be good. I've seen them in action; I know their work; and I know they don't produce garbage.

I can't say what a product has done *for me* if I haven't used it. But I can say what the product does; I can tell my readers what the person I'm recommending has done; and I can remind them that he hasn't brought out a dud product yet.

Again, this comes down to trust.

For "experience" posts, sales are going to depend on the depth of the connection my audience feels with me. If readers identify with me, like me, and trust me, they'll believe that they'll like the same products that I do.

For these "publisher" posts, readers will buy the affiliate product because they trust my judgment. If I tell them that some publisher has good information and they should listen to that publisher, then many of them will trust me and do it.

Of course, that trust is only going to last as long as it proves to be true. If it turns out that the product is poor or that I've misplaced my own trust in the person I'm recommending, then I can expect my conversion rates to fall through the floor. As that trust dries up, so will my income.

So while these kinds of recommendations are very easy to make, they do carry an element of risk. Choose them carefully and don't promote a product simply to help a friend. A real friend will understand why you have to refuse if you're not 100 percent certain that the product is going to deliver.

A third kind of recommendation is the type that just lets people know about a product and tells them that it looks cool. These are probably the most popular, if only because they're the easiest.

If you see a book, a gadget, or a tool that you'd like to buy, you can just write a post telling people about it. Include an affiliate link, and some people will click through and pay.

Clearly, the conversion rate will be lower than it would be for a product you can recommend personally or one that has been created by someone you can recommend personally, but you should be able to generate a few sales and give yourself a little extra income.

The number of sales you generate though will also be affected by its placement, our next topic of discussion.

PLACEMENT

I first saw the potential of the Internet when I realized that moving my ad units from one place on the page to another sent my click-through rate through the roof. Content was important, of course, but it was how I implemented the ads that had the most immediate effect on my returns.

It's no surprise then that placement and implementation have a massive influence on affiliate earnings, too.

When you're working with ad units, there's a lot to experiment with. You can play with the color schemes and fonts. You can try different keywording to see which terms bring up the best ads. And you can use various sizes to see which are most likely to attract readers' eyes. It's a process, and although there are now guidelines that make the testing stage shorter than it used to be, you can still expect to spend a few weeks trying out different strategies to see what works best on your site.

For affiliate ads, it's all much simpler.

Text links outperform banner ads, and links worked into the content outperform links placed in navigation sections.

The difference is remarkable, and it really does prove that simplicity is best. At least one blogger has found that simply swapping his affiliate banner ad for a text link increased his click-throughs by 60 percent. Others have seen even more dramatic improvements with equally simple changes.

Big merchants like Amazon offer a giant range of different types of ad units (including contextual versions that try to read the content on your page and offer products to match, such as AdSense). They're all very neat and snazzy, but rarely do they perform as well as simply linking a key phrase in the content to the product and including your affiliate code (Figure 5.4).

Figure 5.4 Amazon offers a giant range of product links, banners, and widgets to attract users and win sales. But recommended text links will always do best.

The reasons are pretty clear.

First, a text link looks natural. A banner ad looks like an ad, so although it's more likely to be seen than subtle hyperlinked text, it's less likely to be clicked. Users feel that they can happily ignore ads, but when the publisher has taken the effort to link directly to a web site, that link appears to be recommended. It looks like additional information to the content on the page, something that's worth reading.

The text around the link also leads users to click. It puts the product in context and raises curiosity. Having read about the product, the user is likely to want to click through and see the product itself.

Text links also make for cleaner Web pages. Instead of a page filled with flashing graphics that serve mostly to drive users away, the user will be able to see a page designed primarily to serve content. The ad will be embedded inside that content.

That doesn't mean that affiliate graphic ads never pay. In fact, while you can expect your text links to dramatically outperform affiliate graphic ads, the best strategy is often to combine different methods to increase the chances of winning click-throughs and sales. In the sample post I provided earlier for example, I would expect most of the affiliate sales to come from the text link containing my affiliate code. However, I would also use an affiliate image of the product to illustrate the post.

I'm going to want a graphic element there anyway to attract eyes, so using an affiliate ad from Amazon or even linking an image with my affiliate code provides one more way for users to learn more about the product—and gives me another chance to generate a KaChing.

It's also possible to place affiliate ad units on the page. Just don't expect them to generate more clicks than a conventional CPC ad unit while earning money only for those that convert into sales. In general, that's more likely to happen on sites such as AppCraver, ones that discuss products.

The position on the page isn't as important as it might seem, either. When you're using Kontera, you'll want to put some effort into ensuring that the ads aren't sent down to the bottom of the page where no one will see them. But Kontera gives you no direct control over which terms are linked. When you're inserting your own affiliate links, you get to choose where to put the links and more important, you get to write the text that surrounds those links.

Affiliate advertising gives you complete control.

Clearly, placing the affiliate link on the last word on the page is always going to be a bad idea, but it's unlikely to matter whether it appears in the first, second, or fifth paragraph—provided the preceding text has generated enough interest and enough enthusiasm to persuade readers to click through.

SEND AFFILIATE E-MAILS

Spam has caused a huge amount of damage. According to Ferris Research, the global cost in lost productivity caused by unsolicited, unwanted e-mails was an incredible $130 billion in 2009. All that time spent deleting e-mails and flicking through folders looking for lost messages adds up.

It's no surprise then that those offers of herbal pills and fake watches have had an effect on legitimate direct mail marketing. Comparing figures produced each year by the Direct Marketing Association (DMA) reveals that between 2006 and 2009, as the volume of spam shooting around the Internet continued to set new records, the return on investment for e-mail promotions fell by about 25 percent. That sounds like a marketing strategy in trouble . . . until you look at the figures a little more closely.

In 2006, according to the DMA, every dollar spent creating and sending an e-mail with a promotional offer generated $57.25 in return. By 2009, that ROI had fallen to $43.62. *But that's still twice the amount earned from search-based advertising.* (By way of comparison, the ROI of traditional, mailed catalogs was estimated at just $7.32.)

The reason spammers continue to send out billions of e-mails every year is that even their irritating, scattergun approach delivers profits. E-mail advertising works, and it works better than any other form of marketing on the Web.

Spam, though, has frightened people off. According to the DMA, marketers spent $600 million on e-mail advertising in 2009. That's just a fraction of the $11.2 billion spent on search advertising, even though it delivered only half the KaChing for the buck. That means that marketers who know how to practice e-mail marketing, who understand how to do it in a way that delivers information about quality products to people who have chosen to receive that information, can make the most of a massive opportunity.

Proper e-mail marketing isn't difficult to do. Even the law provides a bit of help.

The CAN-SPAM Act of 2003 threatens fines of $11,000 for each unsolicited e-mail delivered to each recipient. Considering the number of recipients in each spam campaign, that should be a hefty threat. Officials have occasionally handed out the odd giant fine, collecting piles of cash and confiscating Porsches from unlucky spam artists. But most spammers feel—for good reason—that they're never going to be caught, so they keep sending out the messages. The act might not be very helpful at keeping out spammers, but it does provide useful guidelines that everyone marketing through e-mail should understand and follow. You can think of them as rules for good e-mail business, and they cover three areas:

1. *Unsubscribe compliance.* Every marketing e-mail you send has to have a way for recipients to pull themselves off your list, and those requests have to be honored within 10 days. Usually that

just means an e-mail link at the bottom of your message marked "unsubscribe."

2. *Content compliance.* "From" lines and subject lines have to be relevant, and you have to include your physical address, not just your e-mail address, in the message.

3. *Sending behavior compliance.* This requirement is designed to clamp down on the most deceptive behavior. It prohibits sending e-mail through open relays to harvested e-mail addresses and using a false header. Those are the kinds of things that only a real spammer would do and they don't affect legitimate e-mail marketers.

These requirements are the minimum, and there are no restrictions against e-mailing existing customers or people who have inquired about your products. CAN-SPAM calls these "relationship" messages, and they're perfectly legitimate.

In practice, legitimate e-mail marketers go further than CAN-SPAM's rules. They use "double opt-in" lists. Subscribers have to click a button declaring that they agree to receive marketing messages from you. They then receive a confirmation e-mail that they have to click again before their e-mail address is added to the list.

That makes it impossible for someone to add someone else's e-mail address to a list maliciously, and it also makes it impossible for anyone to say that they shouldn't be on the list. If that sounds like you're putting a pile of hurdles in front of people you'd like to be marketing to, understand that it's a practice that benefits marketers as much as recipients. It ensures that the e-mail addresses on your list are functional and accurate, and it reduces the bounce rate when you send out your messages. You don't need to be a programming genius to use this system, either. Mass mailing services often provide free scripts to their customers. SendBlaster (www.sendblaster.com), for example, supplies a simple PHP script that you can upload to your server and explains in five steps how to use it (Figure 5.5). It's very simple, and most decent mass-mailing systems supply a toolbox for their clients to use. They want to make your e-mail marketing easy so that you'll become a subscriber. It's a good deal.

Of course, you still have to build your list, but part of your Internet business strategy should consist of picking up e-mail addresses whenever possible. You're going to be handing out lots of free samples, reports, and white papers to bring people to your web site and spread your name around the Web. The price for those should always be an e-mail address that allows you to send them information about products they might want to buy in the future.

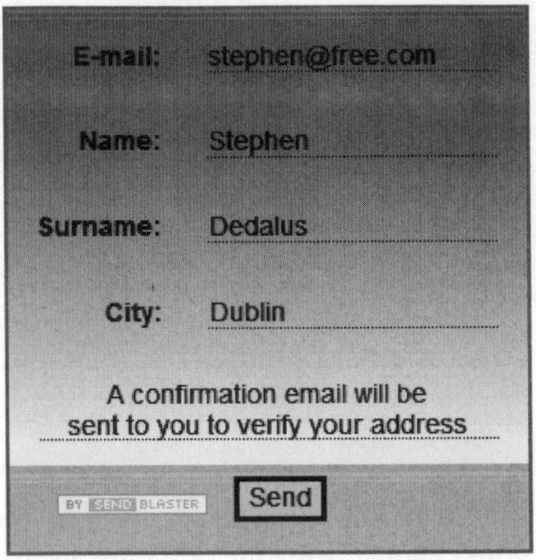

Figure 5.5 SendBlaster helps you build a double opt-in system in seconds.

Thousands of people are going to flow through your web site every month. You want to make sure that they're leaving with a hook that enables you to pull them back at a later date.

When you're signing them up, you'll also have an opportunity to push other products in their direction. If someone has shown enough interest in the information you're providing to give you their e-mail address, then some of them will be interested in other free information, too. People who sign up for the free copy of my AdSense Secrets e-book, for example, have to leave their e-mail address. They're then taken to a "thank you" page that advises them to check their spam filters for their confirmation message. The bottom half of the page is an advertisement for a free trial of my *Top One Report* newsletter.

Enough people sign up for that report to more than cover the cost of the free books that I'm handing out.

In effect, I'm using an information product to grow my e-mail list, and at the same time, I'm signing up paying subscribers to a publication. All it's costing me is free copies of my e-book.

It really doesn't take a great deal of effort to produce a free information product, place it online, and capture e-mail addresses of people who want to enjoy it.

As you build your list, you'll want to make sure that it's managed well. Or rather, you'll want to make sure that *they're* managed well, because the more products you make available, the more lists you'll create. Those lists are likely to be for products about similar subjects—someone who downloads a report on low-cost home repairs, for example, may also download an e-book on home carpentry—so you can send the same marketing information about similar products to different lists.

When you have that kind of overlap, it's a good idea to make sure that you're not sending the message to the same recipient more than once. It's easy to do, and it's the kind of thing that quickly pares down your lists, as people make use of that unsubscribe link.

So what should you be sending to the people on your list?

Affiliate marketing by e-mail is different from affiliate marketing online. Your visitors see your Web page only after *choosing* to visit your site. An e-mail is presented to someone who has *not* come to you; you've come to them with a product you think they're going to like.

It's the difference between store assistants who ask shoppers how they can help and people who hand out flyers on the street. Shoppers are willing to listen; passersby—even those looking in your shop window—will give you only a second of their time. You'll have to work fast to keep them interested and lead them into the store.

That means e-mail messages that contain affiliate links tend to be more "sales-y" than Web content. The risk, of course, is that a subscriber who receives a sales message will glance at it and make a beeline for the unsubscribe link.

That's fine. If subscribers don't want to be bothered by sales messages, if they don't want to know about the products that I've chosen to offer them, then there's no reason for me to continue sending them e-mails. They aren't going to buy, so I don't want to annoy them. I'd rather send messages to 100 people who are interested in buying than to 1,000 who have no interest at all.

Every time I send an e-mail to my subscriber list then, I expect to receive a number of unsubscribe requests. Those numbers tend to be lower than you might expect—that's the benefit of double opt-ins and offers of good products—and I keep track of the numbers. If an offer results in a higher than average number of unsubscribe requests, I'll make a note not to offer that kind of product again. Not only are my subscribers not interested in buying it, they don't want to see it, either. The response I receive tells me something about my subscribers and the information they're looking for.

Unfortunately, much of that information will be negative. Let's say, for example, that a marketer I know tells me that he's created a kit that allows web site publishers to create terms and conditions pages automatically. The product looks good, I trust the publisher, and I think the information will help my subscribers solve a real problem.

I send it out with an affiliate link. One of two things is going to happen. If the product delivers lower than average sales, then it's unlikely I'll be offering another legal product any time soon. I'll understand that my subscribers have found another way to solve those problems, so I won't bother offering them different solutions.

Alternatively, the product could sell at a reasonable 1 to 2 percent conversion rate. If I send the e-mail to 20,000 subscribers, and 1 percent buy a product that sells for $197, then total revenues would be $39,400. If my affiliate cut is one-third, then I will have made just over $13,000. That money will usually come in within two to three days of sending out the message, giving me a very profitable weekend.

Once your Internet business is established, your lists are built up to a good level, and you have cemented relationships with other publishers who have good products, weekends like these become a regular part of your working life.

What do I do next?

I now know that my subscribers have a problem creating their web sites' legal pages. But I've solved that problem. I can't offer a similar product again, even in the hope of reaching the 99 percent of subscribers who didn't buy the first time. If they did not find the first e-mail interesting, nothing brings in those unsubscribes faster than pestering people about the same topic. I might offer other legal products, but it's unlikely that they'll come along too often.

In short, each time you send out an affiliate marketing e-mail, you can never be completely certain what the response is going to be like. But keeping track of previous messages should help you steer clear of the most irritating duds—and writing good, sales-oriented copy should help to ensure that everyone interested in buying does buy. That copy, of course, is vital.

Here is an example of one marketing e-mail that I sent to my subscriber list.

Hi John,

I want to tell you about a new course that's promising to open the world of web site design training right up—and inexpensively, too.

The product's called "The Complete Guide to Web Site Building" and it's from a good friend of mine, Paul Smithson—the guy responsible for XSitePro, the well-respected, award-winning web site design software.

His new course is a monster . . . it's HUGE!!!

In total, it is OVER 30 HOURS long and goes way beyond just building web sites. You'll find everything from how to research your niche to building a list, adding a payment system to a web site, and LOTS more.

There are 26 modules in total, and these are made up of:

♦ Over-the-shoulder demonstrations that lead you by the hand every step of the way

♦ Interactive illustrations that help you to expand your knowledge

♦ Classroom-style lessons that you can watch again and again

(Continued)

(*Continued*)

♦ Quizzes

♦ Homework assignments

=>www.complete-guide-to-website-building.com/go/
page.html

This really is the whole enchilada and then some:-)
It's MASSIVE!
It's principally aimed at people who are newer to web site
design, perhaps people who have:

♦ Tried creating sites with other products like FrontPage,
  Dreamweaver, Expression Web, or Site Build It! only to
  end up giving up out of sheer frustration

♦ Outsourced their web site building up to now

♦ Never even tried creating a site before now

The promise backing the course is as large as the course
itself.
Paul tells me he's going to *personally guarantee* that
the course will deliver ALL the skills you need to create
professional-quality web sites, with a straight 365-day refund
guarantee.
So far, so good. What about price?
You'll often see similar courses retailing for well into four
figures (and for good reason—courses like these take many
months to plan and develop, and they're definitely not cheap
to create) but for some inexplicable reason, Paul's asking for
only $197 for the first 1,000 to sign up, and then the price
shoots up to $297. So don't procrastinate.
Remember, this is the first time Paul has made this available, so I have a feeling once he sees the demand he might want
to rethink that pricing completely! It is DEFINITELY worth a
LOT more!

Here's the link to find out more:
=>www.complete-guide-to-website-building.com/go/
page.html

If you want to kick-start your online empire right now and master the art of web site building, head straight over to the link and check it out. I am sure you'll be VERY impressed, as Paul doesn't do things halfway.

To your success,
Joel Comm

=>www.complete-guide-to-website-building.com/go/
page.html

InfoMedia, Inc., 1151 Eagle Dr. Ste. 325, Loveland, CO 80537, USA

To unsubscribe or change subscriber options visit:
www.aweber.com/z/r/?TOxMbMystCwMLMyMbGwctEa0r
KycTMwsnA

There are a few quick points to note here. The e-mail is addressed to the recipient by first name. You'll be able to capture that information when you ask people to sign up, and the mass mailing program that you use to send out the e-mails will be able to add it automatically. It's much more effective than writing "Dear Subscriber," or even just "Hello."

Again, this is about trust. Subscribers will buy from you if they feel they have a relationship with you. What kind of a relationship is it if you don't even know their name?

That's also why the e-mail has a personal feel. It starts with "I" and is addressed to "you." (And that's "you" singular. Every e-mail and every article you write is read by one person at a time, so address the reader individually.) At one point, it even describes a personal conversation I had with the merchant.

This isn't an ad and it isn't a long-form sales letter. It's a personal message letting people know about a great opportunity. It still has bullet points to describe the features and allow readers to see that this product is meant for them. It identifies the product's unique selling point—its size and comprehensiveness—and it works in the guarantee and the price.

It even creates a sense of urgency by raising the price for people who delay. Of course, the link is isolated so that it stands out and is easy to find. You can also see my company's address at the bottom of the e-mail (above the unsubscribe link). No one has ever stopped by after reading an e-mail like this, but CAN-SPAM says we have to do it.

You'll also notice that the unsubscribe link goes to AWeber (www.aweber.com). This is the company that I use to handle my e-mail marketing campaigns, and it's the one used by most major marketers (Figure 5.6). Although lots of companies offer similar services, AWeber is probably the Microsoft of e-mail marketing software. It's the default option and provides services that are both reliable and flexible enough to handle any campaign.

E-mail marketing might have picked up a bad name, but that reputation isn't completely fair. Double opt-in messages should

Figure 5.6   AWeber really can help with your e-mail marketing. Prices range from $10 per month for 2,500 subscribers to $130 for 25,000. It's not a free service, but the e-mails are effective and worth the money.

form a part of your Internet business and a part of your affiliate strategy, too.

GET THE TIMING RIGHT

Every holiday season, Google brings out a new set of AdSense units. They're in the same formats, and they're all in the usual sizes, but they're decorated with little seasonal pictures. Thanksgiving units might have little illustrations of turkeys; Christmas units could have pictures of Santa or snowmen.

Google does this partly because it likes to be cute. The company uses any excuse to change the Google logo on the search engine home page. It also does this because the company understands the value of timing.

At Christmastime, readers are going to be attracted to a little picture of Santa. They're going to notice the illustration in an ad unit, and instead of looking away, they're going to look closer. And while they're looking, they just might click the ad. The difference isn't huge, but many publishers have reported higher click-through rates after using Google's seasonal ads. (How those ads are implemented though will always be more important.)

Timing is something that affiliates often neglect. It's as though they forget that they're earning money from retailers and completely miss the value of matching products and campaigns to the seasons. It's one of the problems of spending hours in front of a computer: Not only do you forget what day it is, you even forget what time of year it is!

That's a shame, because it's valuable information. The busiest day for Amazon, for example, is exactly 10 days before Christmas.

Most of your affiliate earnings are going to come from writing content that recommends products and inserting text ads into the words. You'll put up the content and watch a percentage of your users click through and buy. Occasionally it pays to prepare and to match your affiliate campaign with the season.

If you know that a large number of people are going to be doing their Christmas shopping on Amazon on December 15, for example, then you could put up a blog post on that day with an affiliate link to a great gift. You could even support that post by including a reference to it and a link in an e-mail sent to your mailing list. Better still, you could hunt down a merchant that you know and trust and negotiate a discount code. That would allow you to create a time-limited offer—exactly the kind of thing that drives sales the most.

Instead of saying, "This product is great, and you should buy it," you'll be able to say, "This product is great, you should buy it, and I've managed to get you a discount. Enter this code within the next two days and you'll save 10 percent."

Because you'll be striking at a time when you know people are planning to buy anyway, as long as the product is good, you should find that you make plenty of sales.

ASK FOR MORE MONEY!

One of the most interesting results that Shawn Collins turned up in his affiliate survey revealed a particularly effective strategy for increasing affiliate earnings ... asking the merchant for a higher affiliate commission.

According to the survey, 58 percent of respondents had successfully asked an affiliate manager for an increase in their commissions. Presumably, many of the 42 percent who said that they hadn't successfully requested an increase hadn't asked for one. Simply getting in touch with your affiliate manager and suggesting that you should be paid more can increase your earnings.

I suspect you'll have to do a little more than say please, though. Affiliate managers are likely to be generous if you can point out how much money you're making for them—and how much more money you could be making for a competitor who has a slightly better program than theirs. Don't beg. Just point out that their program is no longer competitive and that you're making enough money for them that they should keep you on board.

If Shawn Collins's survey is anything to go by, that should be enough to land you higher commissions.

What the FTC's Guidelines Mean for Affiliates

On December 1, 2009, the Federal Trade Commission's new guidelines for endorsements and testimonials in marketing came into force. They've been a long time coming. The rules hadn't been updated for almost 30 years, and a great deal had changed in the marketing world since 1980. The guidelines themselves took a couple of years to put together and were based in part on feedback from marketing and advertising associations, as well as consumer organizations. They aren't difficult to read, and there are plenty of examples that make reasonably clear what you can and can't do. As with any legal document that affects me, I asked my lawyer, Kevin Houchin, to look over it and give me his opinion.

What he said was both fascinating and important.

The guidelines concern the way that endorsements and testimonials are used in advertising, and they are intended to ensure that advertising isn't misleading or dishonest. That's fair enough. There are 16 new rules, but Kevin identified two that are going to have the biggest effect on marketers, especially affiliate sellers.

GENERALLY EXPECTED PERFORMANCE

The first is the issue of *generally expected performance.*

This goes to the heart of why we place testimonials in sales letters. We want leads to understand that they too can enjoy the success that other customers have had using the product. That's why whenever someone sends me an e-mail telling me how much their AdSense income went up as a result of reading the AdSense code, or how many followers they picked up after using my Twitter strategies, I know I have a valuable asset that can help me build trust. I can put that testimonial in my sales material and prove that my product works.

People have used it, and these were their results. If you use it, you can have these results, too.

And that's where the problem begins. Testimonials are meant to be inspirational. They're supposed to show leads what it's *possible* to achieve using your products. The most powerful testimonials always come from the outliers, the people who put every one of your strategies to work, who thought about what they were doing, and who burned the midnight oil to put it all together.

But these people are not typical. I know that when I sell a product—or even when I recommend a product to my readers—they aren't all going to make full use of the ideas that the product contains. Some will, and they'll have great results. Many will implement *some* of the strategies, and they'll get results, too. Some, though, will do nothing. The book will sit on their desk, get covered in papers, and achieve nothing more than make their workspace a little messier.

When I put up testimonials, I don't want to pick the average results because that average score will be brought down by all the people who didn't do anything to build their success. I want to pick the best testimonials, the ones that tell people what's possible if they're prepared to put in the effort. Those are the ones that describe just how much life *can* change once they've bought my product. The results might not be typical, but they are *possible*.

The new FTC guidelines say I can't do that. They state that the endorsement must describe what buyers "will generally achieve." In the past, we could have gotten around that by putting up a best-case testimonial, then adding in small type underneath, "Results not typical." Not anymore. The FTC states specifically that this kind of provision isn't strong enough to overcome the impression that the result in the testimonial is average.

In other words, if you sell an information product that teaches knitting enthusiasts how to sell their creations and someone writes back to you saying that after buying your book, they've managed to earn a five-figure monthly income, give up their day job, and live the life they've always dreamed of . . . you can't use it.

That sounds like a terrible waste, so Kevin Houchin came up with a number of other options. One was to wing it. The FTC has to prove that your advertising is misleading, and that's not going to be easy to do. Before the FTC attorneys go through all the hassle of launching a court case, they'll send warnings asking you to change the advertising copy. That's one option, but it's not the best.

Alternatively, you can do what the FTC wants you to do. It wants you to use testimonials that reflect typical results, and to be able to produce evidence that those results are typical.

So before your launch, you could hand out samples to a representative number of people. Ask them to use the product and tell you the results. Collect testimonials from everyone, and use the responses that reflect the average results. You can also ask a market research firm to do this work for you.

That's worth doing in any case. It will give you valuable insight into the effectiveness of your product. But it's slow work; it might be expensive (especially if you're using a market research firm); and it still makes using your very best testimonials difficult, because those won't be typical. The FTC states:

[I]f the advertiser does not have substantiation that the endorser's experience is representative of what consumers will generally achieve, the advertisement should clearly and conspicuously disclose the generally expected performance in the depicted circumstances, and the advertiser must possess and rely on adequate substantiation for that representation.

So you *could* use that great testimonial, but you'd have to explain afterward what most people actually achieve and have the evidence to prove it. Consider the following testimonial:

> *Since reading "Make Money with Knitting," sales of my woolen sweaters have added two zeros to my income! I now make $12,000 a month selling my knitwear. I've given up my teaching job and knit on the deck of my beach house in Cancún.*
> **—Jane Smith, Owner, Knitwear, Inc.**

If you used this, immediately after it you'd have to add:

"Most knitters who used these strategies saw increases of at least 12 percent."

That's not terrible and using "at least" does allow you to show that there is room for buyers to do better, but it does show that your best-case scenario isn't the one that buyers can typically expect.

Kevin came up with a great idea that allows marketers to use both their best testimonials and the typical results that the FTC wants. Instead of presenting the best results as a *testimonial,* you use them as an *example* of what's possible and explain what the customer did to achieve those results. If the account makes clear that the results are exceptional and not typical, the FTC has no problem with it.

So instead of using the previous (verbatim) testimonial by Jane Smith and qualifying it with the necessary disclaimer (i.e., "Most knitters who used these strategies saw increases of at least 12 percent"), you could write something like this:

Jane Smith's Story

In September 2009, Jane Smith had just about given up hope. She'd been knitting for almost 20 years and had been selling her sweaters, scarves, and gloves online for almost 2 years, but she'd never earned more than $120 a month in revenue.

"I was just about ready to give up," she says. Within just six months of using the strategies in "Make Money with Knitting," though, Jane's revenues rocketed to $12,000 a month. She's since sold her studio apartment and now knits from her beach house in Cancún.

How did Jane create her dream life?

Jane did three things that massively boosted her income.

♦ She created an entirely new range of knitwear products. (We explain how to do that in Chapter 3—"Creating Novelty Knitwear Products.")

♦ She created unique sales pages for her best-selling items (Chapter 6—"Building Sales Pages That Sell.")

> ♦ And she leveraged her friends and family, used social media to build a brand, and managed to put her items in stores across the country.
>
> All of those actions, together with her dedication, hard work, and her amazing designs, enabled Jane to boost her business and turn her passion for knitting into a six-figure income.

As far as the FTC is concerned, the details in the description should be enough to show that the results are specific to Jane and not typical of customers as a whole. It's the difference between a testimonial that says, "After drinking two weight-loss shakes a day for six months, together with diet and exercise, I lost 110 pounds," and one that says, "Every day, I drank two WeightAway shakes, ate only raw vegetables, and exercised vigorously for six hours at the gym. By the end of six months, I had gone from 250 pounds to 140 pounds." That's the example of a fair testimonial supplied by the FTC.

A description like this doesn't just meet the FTC's requirements, it also brings to life what your product can do. It makes your testimonials a little more human, and that's not a bad thing at all.

In practice, I think we'll find that marketers are going to respond to the FTC in a number of different ways. Some, no doubt, will ignore the new guidelines and continue in their old ways, at least until they get a letter suggesting that they're in trouble. Certainly, there are going to be lots of old sales letters on the Web that were written before the new guidelines and haven't been updated.

Many will do what the FTC wants and put up their best testimonials with a rider pointing out the *typical* results.

And some—the smart ones, perhaps—will turn their best testimonials into detailed stories.

Transparency

The other issue that Kevin highlighted concerns *transparency*.

The FTC feels that if you're recommending a product, and you're earning money from the sale of that product, buyers should know that you have a vested interest.

That sounds reasonable, but in practice it's hard to imagine that buyers aren't already aware of affiliate connections. Affiliate links don't look like standard HTML links: They contain the affiliate code, which is a bit of a giveaway. I doubt that anyone who receives my marketing e-mails isn't fully aware that, in addition to these products being carefully chosen and recommended by me, I have an affiliate relationship with the seller. If I think a product is good, of course I'll want to cash in on it. And if I don't think a product is good, I won't want to go near it.

A number of publishers go even further by adding "(aff)," short for "affiliate" after the link, to let everyone know that they earn from a purchase. That's been common practice for years, and it might well be something we'll all have to get used to doing, even if it might put off the odd buyer whose eyes wander to the term in brackets instead of focusing on the link.

It's important to remember that the FTC's rules are guidelines and difficult to enforce. The best strategy is to show that you're doing everything you can to be in compliance and to market fairly.

Affiliate selling has now become a traditional part of Internet marketing. It can earn giant amounts of cash for you, or it can add nothing more than a pleasant extra KaChing to a site that brings in money in a number of other ways. Used carefully, on a site with plenty of traffic and a close connection with readers, and it can be a hugely valuable and simple way to deliver income.

Membership Sites—Turning Your Internet Business into a Passive Revenue Machine

One of the biggest challenges in marketing is the fact that it's never-ending. Making profits means making lots of sales, but at the end of every sale, you have to return to the marketplace and find another buyer.

There are things that you can do of course to bring your old buyers back. Newsletters, e-mail marketing, and a constant flow of good content will all keep attracting those buyers and ad clickers. But each time you send out one of those e-mails or put up a new post, you still have to persuade users to buy a product or click on an ad. Internet marketing is a constant process of attracting, selling, and converting.

Wouldn't it be great if every time you converted a lead into a customer, those customers agreed to pay again and again, without fail, every single month?

Instead of wondering how much you're going to earn each month, you'd know that your subscribers will give you a set amount of money. Your business would have a firm financial foundation, allowing you to focus your efforts on creating new products that can bring in large, immediate bursts of cash to supplement that steady flow. Create a system in which the products your subscribers buy are created and distributed by staff or freelancers, and you'll even have a high-paying *passive* revenue stream.

That's what this chapter teaches you to do. It explains what membership sites are, what they should offer, how to price your subscriptions, what you have to do to keep your subscribers, and how to set the whole thing up without giving yourself a migraine.

What Is a Membership Site?

Continuity programs are as old as newspaper subscriptions—probably older. Members sign up for a product or a service and are billed on a regular schedule as long as they want to enjoy the benefits of that product or service. It's the model that's allowed the print media to become an established business. It keeps TV programs flowing through your cable box, ensures that you remain connected to the Internet through your Internet service provider, lets you talk on your mobile phone, and has even allowed *Reader's Digest* and others to create book clubs to deliver novels you never read to your doorstep every month.

Programs like these have proven their success on the Internet, too. Although newspapers and other content sites have struggled to persuade readers to pay to read their products, sites that offer services have become a multi-million-dollar industry. The online dating industry, for example, is predicted to be worth $932 million by 2011 in the United States alone. In Europe, where growth has been more consistent, dating sites are predicted to be worth about 549 million euros by 2011. That's an incredible amount of money, and almost all of it is coming in month after month on a regular basis.

Members of these sites sign up, enter their credit card details, agree to pay their monthly retainer, and in return are granted access to parts of the site that nonmembers can't reach. While those nonmembers are confronted with a pay wall when they try to access the site, members are waved through after entering their username and password. Once inside, they can view complete profiles, send and receive messages, and chat online with potential dates. Their membership makes them feel like part of an exclusive club and lets them enjoy all of the benefits and features that come with club membership.

The sites, for their part, work hard to ensure that as few people as possible cancel (at least not until they've found the love of their life) and that their members get the benefits they're paying for.

The principle itself isn't complex, and it's likely to be one that you benefit from every day. As long as the benefits keep flowing toward the customer—whether that's in the form of information, entertainment, or networking—the funds will continue flowing toward the seller. The key is to understand which benefits Internet users are willing to pay for.

What Do Online Membership Sites Have to Offer?

It might seem surprising that sites like Match.com and eHarmony are doing so well. While those sites have millions of members, there are also plenty of free dating sites on the Web that make their money through advertising. Anyone can join them, anyone can view the profiles, and anyone can send and receive messages and browse the site for potential dates. Some of those sites are doing very well. But none of them are doing well enough to pose a real threat to the market's leaders—all of whom charge a monthly fee.

That isn't true for other sectors. At the moment, only a few content sites have successfully managed to charge people to view their articles, and those sites tend to be in the finance sector. The *Wall Street Journal* demands just over $100 for an annual subscription to its web site, delivering only short previews to nonsubscribers (although subscribers can send articles to their friends, allowing the publication to benefit from viral marketing). The *Economist* asks for about $90.

These kinds of sites—dating sites that demand a membership fee and news sites that demand a paid subscription—are offering something that users are clearly prepared to pay for. In the case of dating sites, that's *exclusivity*.

When they can pick up the same service on a free dating site, members see the pay wall as a filter keeping out people who aren't serious. If someone is prepared to dip into their pocket to pay a $25-a-month subscription fee, then that's a great sign that they mean business. They're less likely to be looking for a short-term relationship and more likely to be active on the site and prepared to invest in building a new relationship with someone they meet online. They're also likely to be financially stable enough to afford the membership fee—a decent sign that they'll make a good date!

For readers of the *Wall Street Journal*'s online edition, the return is *value*. Subscribers may well feel that the content available on the site does more than satisfy their curiosity; it gives them professional information that's worth more than the price they're paying for it. The knowledge that they gain by reading the paper's reports every day, for example, may give them a better understanding of what's happening on the stock exchange, thus helping them to make smarter investments, which will in turn bring in more money than the $100 subscription fee.

Create a site that offers either a sense of exclusivity similar to that found on Match and eHarmony, or provide the kind of high-value content offered by publications like the *Wall Street Journal,* deliver it to them in a steady, undisturbed flow, and you should be able to persuade your users to pay you every month, too.

Those are the principles that have allowed my own membership site to grow and prosper. The Profit Vault (www.TheProfitVault .com) is a membership site that doles out valuable training and content to my members over a 13-week period. For those who want to learn practical strategies for making money online, we've organized our content in a consumable manner that provides weekly objectives, motivation, instruction, and action items so that users can pursue their online goals. Members pay $47 per month to enjoy this content (Figure 6.1).

The Profit Vault is an online example of a membership site or continuity program. But that doesn't mean you can't create physical products and receive recurring payments from customers.

One of our popular offline products is the *Top One Report* (www.TopOneReport.com). As a magazine format, this publication offers fresh, original content written by me and members of my

Figure 6.1   The Profit Vault is an example of a membership site that people will gladly pay for on a recurring basis. As long as you are providing value, customers are all too happy to continue subscribing.

staff. We tackle all things business-related, with a special focus on online business. But unlike a typical magazine subscription, the *Top One Report* commands a premium of $29.95. Just as people will pay more for an e-book that provides instant gratification and valuable material, our subscribers are willing to pay more for our report because of the quality of the information found within. Remember, it's all about providing value. If people can justify a purchase that promises a larger ROI than its cost, they will be willing to sign on (Figure 6.2).

That may sound slightly odd: a publication explaining how to make money on the Internet that is produced using old-fashioned ink and paper and dropped in a physical mailbox outside subscribers' homes.

Of course, I could put all of the content in the *Top One Report* online. I could post it on a web site, and I could distribute it by PDF. But there are a couple of reasons I don't do that.

The first is piracy. This content is exclusive. People have paid for it and I want them to continue doing so. If I put it online and charge for it, I can be sure that some copies will be e-mailed, shared, and passed around. Some people won't be paying for it. Printed distribution reduces the number of people who are reading my publication for free.

Figure 6.2 Subscription models are nothing new, and sometimes the old way of doing things is still the best. The *Top One Report* is a printed, monthly magazine packed with advice and articles about Internet entrepreneurship.

But a print publication delivers something even more important than piracy protection: It comes with a high perceived value.

Readers expect online content to be free and are unwilling to pay for it. They will, however, pay for magazines, because they assume that the information those magazines contain has been carefully chosen and well researched. Because anyone can create a web site and place content on it, new visitors can never know whether they're about to get some truly valuable information or something that just came off the top of someone's head. A print magazine—like a book—costs money to produce. If someone has decided to invest in that publication, it's a good sign that it contains information that other people are going to find valuable.

In fact, as we'll see, it doesn't cost a great deal to produce a print magazine, and it's possible to do it with no risk at all. But sending out a print publication helps the content contained therein to stand apart from information online. It increases the odds that people will read it and take it seriously.

Pricing Your Membership: How Much Is Too Much?

Setting a price for a product usually means coming up with a number that's both as high as possible and one that attracts as many people as possible. When you're setting a price for a club membership, the philosophy is a little different.

You want a price that puts people off.

Obviously, you don't want to put *everyone* off. An empty subscription site isn't going to make a great deal of money for you. But you want a price that's high enough to keep out people who aren't completely serious.

That amount is going to vary. According to *Forbes,* when Sebonack Golf Club opened in 2006, the initiation fee for new members was said to be a record $650,000. Today, it is rumored to have reached seven figures. Those prices guarantee that the person sitting next to you at the eighteenth hole is equally important, equally successful, equally interesting . . . and equally rich. If you have to ask how much membership costs, then it's probably not for you. Other golf clubs might not require that their members hand over checks for $1 million, but most have fees that are designed to strike a balance between attracting new members and putting off people who might cause current members to head for the door.

On the other hand, even a small fee can be effective. Elance extracts a service fee of between 4 and 6 percent on every job outsourced on the site. With over $235 million already earned by providers, even at 5 percent, the company would have pulled in almost $12 million. But Elance also requires that providers pay a monthly subscription fee that ranges from $9.95 for individuals to $39.95 for businesses.

Surely it would be in Elance's interest to have as many providers listed as possible. The more providers the site has bidding for jobs, the greater the choices for buyers.

That's the problem. Buyers don't want to choose between hundreds of applicants for a job they post. They want to choose between a handful of highly qualified and experienced professionals. Providers want to make clear that they are professionals who take their work seriously. That 10-buck fee keeps out people who have no qualifications at all and who feel that they have nothing to lose by writing a pitch. It helps to maintain the quality of Elance's providers—and it also gives the site some additional revenue from providers who are too busy to bid regularly or who rarely win jobs.

So how do you set a price for your membership site?

There are a number of factors you have to consider. As always, competition will be one, but subscription sites are an underexploited opportunity. Unless you're creating a club for singles—in which case, you'll have lots of company—there's a good chance that you'll find that your site is the only one of its kind in your field.

That means you'll need to think about value, and you'll need to think about the services you're offering. Most important, you'll need to think about the return that your members are going to be receiving for their monthly subscription. They don't have to get that return every month—and you don't have to charge every month if you don't want to. Newspapers and magazines often take an annual fee. New subscribers are at their most enthusiastic when they first sign up. As they see the money dripping out of their account every month, there's always the chance that they'll cancel. They are less likely to do that in the middle of an annual subscription period, and they are more likely to renew at the end of it, too.

But if your subscription site supplies information, contacts, or services worth $1,000, for example, then demanding $20 a month looks like a steal.

Of course, measuring those returns is never easy, so review the information products in your field. Think of your subscription site as offering the equivalent of one relevant e-book per month and try charging a rate similar to the price you'd charge for that e-book. There's no scientific formula here, but if buyers in your field are known to pay $70 for an e-book that they understand will deliver solid returns, then there's a good chance that they'll pay a similar amount for membership in a club that promises similar returns from the same kind of information.

If you find the price is too high, it's always easy enough to lower it. Declare that you're slashing the price for a limited time, and not only will you be able to adjust the subscription fee downward until it reaches the right level, you'll also have the chance to create the kind of time-limited offers that bring quick results.

Creating Your Membership Site the Easy Way

Subscription sites look fairly complex. They're filled with all sorts of valuable features: content pages, members' profile pages, groups, internal messaging, and all sorts of other useful things that help members to network and learn. You can even include multimedia content and training videos.

Consequently, they have to be hard to build, right? They have to be expensive to create, difficult to plan, and a real challenge to design, launch, and put together, don't they?

Not a bit of it.

At the beginning of this book, I pointed out that the Internet has now developed to the point where proven revenue generators have become automated. Web site publishing can be done by picking a domain name, choosing a template, and filling in the gaps with your own pictures and text.

Blogging is even easier. Automated programs let you go from user to publisher, posting your first online blog in less than five minutes. The next day, once Google has approved your AdSense application, you could even be seeing your first advertising income.

Creating membership sites is now just as simple. A bunch of different programs are available on the Web that mean you don't have to know anything about coding, designing, or planning to be able to launch your site. You don't even have to hire a programmer or a designer to do all of the hard work for you. It's easy enough to do yourself.

One of those programs is SubHub.com (Figure 6.3). Created by Miles Galliford, an expert on digital content, the site offers a bunch of different features that allow publishers to charge a subscription fee or even to offer pay-per-view videos. According to Miles's own Squidoo page, a subscription site should include:

♦ Secure premium content

♦ A searchable database of members' data

♦ Password control, including the ability to disable the password at the end of the subscription period, notice when a

Figure 6.3   SubHub (www.subhub.com) lets you build and manage a subscription–supported web site from one place. Think of it as combining the ease of blogging with the revenues of a paid site.

single password is being shared among different users, and automatically remember returning members

♦ Payment integration, including regular billing

♦ Autoresponders that send out messages after sign-up, before renewals, and so on

♦ An easy-to-use control panel

It's no surprise to find that his own platform offers all of these things, as well as search engine optimization, the ability to include AdSense units and affiliate links, a way to sell information products from inside the site, and a range of templates to choose from.

SubHub is not the only service offering the ability to create membership sites easily. WildApricot (www.wildapricot.com) is really geared toward helping nonprofits and clubs create member sites, but it can be used to build subscription sites as well. With fees that begin at $25 per month (although the $50 option offers more useful features), it's not terribly expensive, but the sites can look a little cheap, too. At $97 per month, SubHub is almost twice the price, but the sites created *do* appear professional—and are worth paying for.

GrowingforMarket.com (www.growingformarket.com) was created using SubHub. The site, which provides information for farmers, offers three different subscription levels. Online subscribers can download a PDF of each new edition of the magazine; "full-access members" can also access the archive; and "full-access-plus" subscribers receive a printed copy of the magazine each month.

Note that there are no community features on this site. SubHub simply allows the publication to restrict access to its content and charge a rate that starts at $30 per year. Assuming that the site is paying an annual discounted fee to use SubHub, it wouldn't need to sell more than 33 subscriptions to cover the hosting, building, and maintenance costs. When you're supplying key information to a tightly niched market, it's possible to do that with content alone.

When you're looking to build a membership site, there are plenty of other options around as well, including MemberWing (www.memberwing.com), a WordPress plug-in that lets publishers hide their premium content behind a pay wall. It's also possible, of course, to create all of these features yourself. The advantages are that you won't have to use one of the templates the platform provides and you'll have complete flexibility about the site's look, feel, and layout. If you're handy with Dreamweaver and know what to do with PHP, then it shouldn't take you too long. If you have the cash and want to hire someone to do it for you, it shouldn't be beyond the skills of most decent PHP programmers.

A platform like SubHub will give you the site, complete with the protected content, membership forums, and all of the other things you'll need to persuade people to sign up and pay. But what if you want a print magazine like the one I send to subscribers of my *Top One Report*?

One option is to do what GrowingforMarket does: Create a PDF version of the magazine and place it behind the pay wall. It's simple, and because there are no production or delivery fees, you can charge a small amount for it. In effect, you're creating a different kind of blog, one with the format and layout of a traditional magazine. You won't get the piracy protection, though. While PDF documents do have some level of protection, they can always be shared, e-mailed, and passed around.

In addition, they don't have the perception of value that comes with a print publication, nor do they have the same ease of reading—which is why even GrowingforMarket charges more to send a copy of its publication to its subscribers' physical mailboxes.

Creating a print publication doesn't have to be difficult or expensive. While it's always possible to work with a local printer who can run off copies for you, that can be expensive, especially for small print runs. Laying out the publication each month can be time-consuming, and you'll still have to cope with changes in your subscriber list—which happens often, especially as your list grows. If you're lucky, and you can work the extra cost into the price of the subscription, you might find that your local printer is also willing to address the envelopes, add the postage, and mail them for you. That should help to save you—or your assistants—some unpleasant work each month.

Again, though, much of the tricky stuff has now been simplified with automated online systems. One option is to use MagCloud (www.magcloud.com), a service created and run by Hewlett-Packard. You can create your magazine using any design program you want, upload it to the site, and receive a proof copy to review. Once it's approved, the magazine is added to MagCloud's store and is available for sale on a print-on-demand basis. The cost for publishers is 20 cents per page, but publishers get to set the sale price, so any rate above 20 cents is profit.

Don't expect too many one-off sales just by listing your magazine on the web site, though. Promoting MagCloud's store isn't the best way to market your magazine. Instead, use the site's bulk orders feature. You'll be able to mail in your subscriber list and send the magazine to all of your subscribers automatically. Once the number of copies printed reaches 20, the cost falls by 20 percent. You're billed for the printing costs, but if you're collecting the subscription fees automatically anyway, that shouldn't be a problem. You'll have the cash.

The result will be a magazine of, say 24 pages, that costs $3.60 plus shipping to produce.

Those are just the printing and production costs. The real work comes in writing, design, and layout. Although a printed publication and a blog are just two ways of delivering information, the format of the information is very different. Readers have less patience online, so they're more likely to read short posts of 1,000 words or even less. Magazines tend to have three different sections, each with content of different lengths. The front-of-book section might have an editor's introduction, then news summaries describing events in your field. It's supposed to pull readers in and spark their interest before they move on to the features.

Those features are the meat of the magazine, the place where subscribers will really feel they're getting their money's worth. The articles there can be longer than the kinds of posts you might be placing on a web site. They're likely to be more detailed, perhaps include feature interviews or provide clear step-by-step instructions to achieving a goal. Your model will be the kinds of articles you can read in magazines rather than the kinds of posts you can see on web sites.

Finally, the back-of-book section might include columns or reviews—additional content that subscribers might find interesting. Of course, these are just guidelines. It's always possible to mix things up and decide how you want your publication to look.

As for the writing—the most important part of your magazine—creating an entire magazine by yourself is likely to be too difficult and take up too much of your time. You will need to outsource the writing to members of your team, to professional freelance writers, or to guest contributors who are experts in your field. You should find that many people are willing to contribute for free, as a way of putting their own name and expertise in front of your readers, but it's not difficult to work out how much you can afford to pay for regular contributions of features or columns. It's still best to hand over the general management of the publication to someone on your staff. Creating the kind of magazine that actually contains the value it appears to offer is a pretty demanding job.

Even that is not as demanding as bringing in subscribers, to both the magazine and your membership web site. Because part of the value of the site will often be the community and its networking opportunities, the site will need a critical mass of members before subscribers will feel they're getting their money's worth. The best option is to focus first on building the community through your blog, Twitter timeline, and other social media channels; only after your traffic reaches a reasonably high level should you open the elite version of your subscription-based community.

Your magazine will be particularly helpful in making the conversions. The standard tactic for bringing in subscribers is to create a low-cost trial that automatically triggers the subscription fee if there's no cancellation. I usually offer a trial of the *Top One Report* for $1, and I make the offer in various locations. It appears at the end of my e-mail newsletters; I tweet it occasionally in my timeline; there's a giant button on my web site that leads to my TopOneReport member page; and, as we've seen, I also talk about it whenever I give away a free information product to help build my mailing list.

The community site tends to appeal more to people I meet and address at conferences. They like the idea of being able to continue talking and exchanging information even after they have left the hotel and headed back home. Much depends on where you're doing the marketing and whom you are marketing to.

Membership sites can be huge revenue generators. If you can set a high monthly fee and bring in enough paying members, you can find that you're running a club that's bringing in tens of thousands of dollars every month and a handsome six-figure income in subscription fees alone. Although the mechanics of creating that site may no longer be difficult, it will require work and expense to build and maintain.

When subscribers are paying a regular fee, they expect to receive full value for those fees every month. Otherwise, you'll find that the number of your subscribers will fall off pretty quickly.

While the writing, editing, and printing are all things you can outsource, a membership site does not offer the same kind of passive revenue as a page of content with an affiliate link or an information product sitting on ClickBank and being promoted by affiliates. New content has to be commissioned, created, edited, and published regularly. And because the time lag between writing, printing, and delivering is so much longer than it is online, the printed publication will need long-term planning and a lead time of at least a couple of months.

Even maintaining the membership site itself, where the members themselves will be doing most of the work, will need plenty of attention.

On the other hand, being the head of a community of paying members can be both incredibly rewarding and remarkably satisfying.

Coaching Programs

At the beginning of this book, I made a confession. I confessed that the success I've enjoyed online wasn't all due to me. Sure, I like to tell myself that even though I might not have invented the Internet, at least I invented Internet marketing, but that's not true, either.

My growth has come by working hard, spotting opportunities, testing different strategies to see which bring the best results, and through determined implementation.

But it's also come by learning from others. Right at the beginning, I hired a business coach who helped me to find the best way to work. I've since hired other coaches who have been able to provide great advice and the benefit of their experience. They've been invaluable whenever I've moved into an area I've never operated in before, and they've certainly more than repaid the fees that I paid them for their suggestions.

That's why once I found that some aspects of Internet marketing were coming easily to me, I was happy to share my knowledge with other entrepreneurs.

Of course, my e-books, my information products, and my web sites were doing that already. But there's always something a little special about being able to meet with the coach, ask questions, and receive answers focused on your particular problem and your specific goals. It's special to the person receiving the information, and it's no less special to the coach. As a coach, I get the satisfaction of being able to interact personally with my audience instead of merely pouring my knowledge onto the page and hoping it's valuable to someone.

It can pay pretty well, too.

While fees can range widely for coaching—from zero at talks where the main benefit is to lead people to buy your products (which, with the right talk can generate some giant sums) to thousands of dollars for just a few days' work—coaching is one of the most lucrative ways for a successful entrepreneur to make money out of his or her expertise.

In this chapter, I explain how, once you've created a successful Internet business, you can move into coaching. First, I explain what coaching is; then I discuss strategies for branding, because who you are is going to be almost as important as what you know.

Then I talk about using PR to get mass impact for your coaching events and explain how to start a low-end coaching program before ramping it up to the high-dollar stuff.

Coaching isn't for everyone. If you're happy building your company by yourself, creating content, marketing products, and forging joint ventures, then that's fine. It's a great way to build a profitable business. But if you do want to give back a little more, then coaching can be both a valuable and a very satisfying way to help others along the path you've created and to cash in on your knowledge.

What Is Coaching?

One of the themes of this book is that your knowledge is valuable. Whether that's professional knowledge built up through years of training and experience or information that you've managed to accumulate by doing what you love, you have an asset that people will pay to own themselves. Blogs, information products, and membership sites are just different channels through which you can deliver that expertise online and receive a fee for it.

Once you've built a successful Internet business, you even create an additional asset that you can market: expertise in creating an Internet business in your field.

Coaching is another way of delivering that information, and it's a particularly intensive and valuable way. For the client, it can bring targeted results, and it embeds the information deeper and faster than any other method.

When people listen to a recording of you explaining how to earn money by uploading video clips to YouTube, some of that information will be missed. If they listen to it while driving to work in the morning, they'll lose concentration every time they have to look at the road. If they've bought your e-book, they'll dip in and out, picking up the information that they think will be the most useful—and leaving plenty of other goodies behind. If they're reading your blog, it's inevitable that they'll miss some of your posts, and besides, blogs aren't the best platform to teach a course. They provide nuggets of information rather than a clear guide from start to success.

Coaching allows people who want to pick up your knowledge direct access to the source. It's the most powerful way of helping people achieve their goals using the knowledge that you've managed to accumulate.

The coaching itself can be done in all sorts of different ways. We've already seen how it's possible to deliver online coaching, either by using specialized software or by creating videos that can be accessed behind a pay wall or delivered on DVD. But coaching is always at its best in person when it's done individually, for a set period of time, or in workshops to a group of people.

Just as the effect of coaching is particularly strong, so the importance of that four-step sales process—know me, like me, trust me, pay me—is concentrated, too.

You don't have to know people very well to start reading their blogs. You need to like them to come back, but if they annoy you occasionally, you can live with it, provided they aren't asking you to do more than browse their content, clicking occasionally on an ad.

You have to like and trust people before you'll buy an affiliate product from them online, but everything has to be firmly in place before they'll hire you as a coach.

You're going to be telling people what they're doing wrong. You're going to be giving them advice related directly to their life, including, perhaps, their personal life, because that's always an influence on professional success, too. They're going to be trusting you with personal information—their doubts, their fears, their dreams for the future—and you're going to have to persuade them that to achieve those dreams they're going to have to do things that they might not want to do.

After all, if they had wanted to do them before now, they would have achieved their success already.

Before people even think about hiring you as a coach, they have to feel that they know you, like you, and absolutely trust you. It's something that can happen only after you've already used your web sites to broadcast who you are.

That identity is presented as your *brand*.

Strategies for Branding

How would you describe yourself? If you had to choose three words that best describe your personality, what would they be?

You might say that you're "loyal, fun-loving, and down-to-earth." Or perhaps you're "adventurous, creative, and caring." Or maybe you're "outgoing, bubbly, and thoughtful."

It's likely that you think you're all of those things together, and if you were to describe yourself completely, you'd probably want to use all of those terms. The people who know you might agree with you, but they'd probably want to highlight one or two in particular. Your friends might find you very funny, for example. Or they might like you because they know you always listen or because you always have such smart advice.

When they think about you, they tend to associate you first with your most obvious characteristic. Whether it's your wit, your big heart, or your giant intelligence, your prime feature helps you to stand out from the people around you.

You can think of that characteristic as your natural brand—and everyone has one. It might not be something you've worked hard to create. It might not be something you've worked at all to create. It's just who are you, and it's how other people have come to see you, and it's how they distinguish you from everyone else they know.

When you're building a coaching business, you'll want to plan and build that brand deliberately. You won't be the only person offering coaching services in your field, and you certainly won't be the only person offering information about your field on your blog and in your products. Your brand will help you to stand out from your competitors. It will help to build a relationship of trust with your audience, and it will show them instantly what they can expect to receive when they join your community.

In the past, branding was mostly restricted to large corporations and specific products. Faced with a shelf full of unfamiliar fizzy drinks, all offering to quench thirst and supply bubbles, Coca-Cola's branding power meant that customers knew what that product would do for them. It wouldn't just refresh them. It wouldn't just give them a sugar rush and a fizzy tongue. If "Coca-Cola is life," then drinking it would give them an instant burst of happiness, energy, and excitement. When choosing between three products whose name you're not familiar with and one you *do* recognize, you'll choose the one you know. Because you're familiar with it, you can trust it to deliver what it says on the bottle.

Branding helps customers confused by a giant range of choices to make smart buying decisions. Especially on the Internet, where the next option is just a click away, it's an essential factor in turning leads into customers and creating a closely knit community that not only returns, but even evangelizes on your behalf.

In the past few years branding has changed. It's become individualized. Now it's possible—even essential—for people to have brands of their own. It's something that's come about through a number of factors. A better understanding of the way branding works is likely to have had much to do with it. We recognize the importance of brands in our own lives, whether it's the Apple logo on our mobile phones, the Nike swoosh on our shoes, or the giant signs that follow each other down the highway. Brands have not only become more commonplace, they've also become recognized. We know what they're doing. We know why they're doing it. And we wonder if the power of branding can do something for us, too.

But the importance of personal branding also has a lot to do with the changes in the job market. Once, it was possible to join a company and know that you would be there until the day you retired. You'd get regular pay raises, earn the odd bonus, and leave with a gold watch and a gold-plated pension. Those days are gone. Companies no longer think twice about cutting employees loose—and the employees think nothing of quitting for another company . . . or setting up shop on their own.

That means we are all responsible for how we appear to buyers, whether those buyers are employers or customers. It means we have to recognize those positive characteristics that help us to stand out and project them so that we're instantly recognizable and never forgotten.

There are two steps to building your brand: (1) understanding the elements your brand should contain and (2) creating the structure that will broadcast that brand.

IDENTIFYING YOUR BRAND

In his book *Me 2.0: Build a Powerful Brand to Achieve Career Success,* branding expert Dan Schawbel talks about the importance of basing a personal brand on authenticity. Brands need to be real, he argues, and should be based on an individual's true character, personality, and outlook. "Why do you need to be real?" he asks. "Because everyone else is taken and replicas don't sell for as much!"

Those are two good reasons, but there's a third that's just as persuasive.

Basing a brand on who you really are is the easiest option available. You won't have to pretend to be someone you're not. You won't risk getting caught out when you talk to people at conferences and workshops. And you won't have to wrack your brain wondering how the person you're trying to project would behave on Twitter, on Facebook, or in your e-books.

You can just relax, be you . . . and make money.

Nor should you have to look too hard to find a unique characteristic that sums up your attitude. It could be your sense of adventure. It could be your head for statistics. It could be nothing more than your winning smile and your positive attitude.

You don't need more than one characteristic to build your brand, and chances are, the first one that comes into your head should be the one you choose.

Psychologists always ask people to say the first thing that comes into their head when they look at a picture. They don't ask for the second thing, and they don't give their subjects time to have a good long think. They want their most immediate reaction—because that's the one that's likely to be the most honest. Ask yourself what you think is the single most outstanding characteristic of your attitude, your personality, or the way you do business, and your first reaction is likely to be the core of your brand.

Obviously, it has to be positive and inspirational. It has to be something that other people would want to have, too. But as long as it's upbeat, fun, and exciting, you should find that it will help you to stand out in the marketplace.

BROADCASTING YOUR BRAND

Much trickier will be broadcasting that brand. This is what giant corporations pay advertising companies suitcase loads of money to do on their behalf. If you have a suitcase or two filled with money that you don't know what to do with, you can save yourself a small headache and do the same thing. There are now plenty of small marketing and branding companies around that will be happy to help make your brand recognizable.

But you don't need a suitcase stuffed with cash to broadcast your brand. One of the advantages of choosing a personal brand that's closely linked to who you really are is that it then becomes very easy to broadcast it yourself. As you'll see, social media has made it easier still.

That's because your brand will consist of two elements: (1) a visual image that is immediately communicated and (2) a style that allows people to feel they're getting close to you and that they know you.

To create the visual image, you'll probably need the help of a professional. A photographer can shoot portraits to use in your marketing material that communicate the characteristic that you most want to put across. You'll have to tell your photographer what

Figure 7.1 "Barefoot Executive" Carrie Wilkerson is an expert on all sorts of marketing topics, but her knowledge of branding comes naturally and serves her well.

you want the image to say. Find someone with the right amount of talent, and you should end up with a selection of photos that you can use for your branding.

Carrie Wilkerson, for example, is a consultant and strategist who helps entrepreneurs who work at home to build their businesses (Figure 7.1). Just look at the main image she uses on her web site BlogBarefoot.com. She's shown sitting on the floor, smiling and relaxed . . . and barefoot.

That's her brand. That's what she's offering to people who hire her as a coach or a consultant. She'll help them to be professional, but in a way that's easy, relaxed, and stress-free. It's a message she communicates through the pictures she uses. It's a feeling that's summarized in the title she uses to describe herself: "The Barefoot Executive." And it's also something that comes across clearly in her Twitter stream (Figure 7.2).

Carrie's tweets are inspiring, positive, and professional, but they're also personal. They help her to communicate her brand and her personality directly to her target market, building a close relationship with people she may well be working with in the future.

Figure 7.2   Carrie Wilkerson's brand name and image help to place her in people's minds. Her tweets help her to build that brand.

Twitter is particularly strong at doing this, and it's another good reason to choose a brand that reflects your true personality. It's very difficult to create a successful timeline that doesn't show who you are. But when your brand is a positive aspect of your personality—your sense of fun, your love of knowledge, your thoroughness—then that will come across naturally in your tweets.

Every time you open your timeline and tell people what you're doing or thinking, you'll be giving your brand another little push and burying it a little deeper in people's minds.

Your personal brand will make you known to your target market. It will help to build trust, and it should lead people to like you. Communicating that brand is a process. It takes time, but as you do it, you should find that it creates a very powerful connection with your audience, encouraging them to return to you . . . and to hire you as a coach, too.

Sometimes you need a tool that will communicate your brand in a way that's much faster, much broader, and much more powerful.

How to Do PR for Mass Impact

Coaching relies on your image as an expert. Students will hire you, sign up for your classes, and buy your coaching videos because they're certain that you know more than they do and more than most people do—and that you can share your knowledge. That expertise will form part of your brand.

Usually, it takes time to build a sense of the depth and value of your expertise. It happens after your blog has been online for a long time and has consistently posted good content. It happens when your information products are bought, shared, passed around, and most important of all, respected.

It happens when you really do know your stuff, and the content that you produce shows that you know your stuff.

But you can take a shortcut to build your brand as an expert: You can get your name in the press.

When reporters are assigned a story, they start looking for sources. They'll want to speak to people who are directly involved in the story. That will give the article a human touch and show the reader that what they're describing does have an impact on people's lives. But they'll also want to speak to an expert. That will explain to the reader what's happening, why it's happening, and why it's important.

Reporters themselves can't do that. They're not the experts. They're just the ones who ask the questions and pass the information on to the reader. They don't create that information themselves. The reader assumes that the experts interviewed by reporters are leaders in their field. The reader assumes that if there were a higher authority on that subject, the reporter would have found and interviewed that person instead.

If you get your name in the press, you'll not only be seen by a huge number of people, those people will also regard you as a leading expert on your topic. When they're thinking about learning how to build a web site, earn money from their illustrations, or create their own babysitting business, you'll be the person they turn to.

Writing press releases is very simple. They're short—about a page in length—and they follow a strict formula:

- Headline

- Introductory paragraph

- Quote

- Two or three informational paragraphs or a series of bullet points

- Final quote

- Blurb about the expert

That's very simple. More difficult is writing the kind of press release that actually wins attention. Reporters receive dozens of press releases every day. Many of them come from companies and PR agencies they know. Others will be sent to them in the vague hope that they'll attract the reporter's attention. Most of them fail.

The reason they fail is usually clear. When business owners write press releases, they tend to think about what the reporter can do for them. They think about how they'll be seen in the report and what effect the publicity will have on their business. What they should be thinking about is what they're going to do for the reporter. They should be producing press releases that contain the kind of story ideas that solve a problem for the journalist: what to write and how to write it. The solution to that problem is a good story idea that entertains the audience and comes complete with expert, contact number, and quotes.

At least, that's the way things used to be. When winning publicity meant picking up a spot in a print newspaper, it was vital to create press releases that were exciting and that stood out. They had to grab reporters' eyes and promise them a solid story that would inform their audiences.

Today, publicity doesn't have to mean a page in the *New York Times* or even exposure via your local newspaper or radio station. It can mean something as simple as a write-up on a blog. That won't deliver as big a pile of prestige as a mention in a major media outlet, but it will still push your name out there and make it known.

That means there are now two ways of writing press releases that win attention.

The first is to write a press release that contains the basic information you want to get across. Following is an example of a press release that I produced when I launched my AdSense Coaching Club.

Google AdSense Expert Announces Premier AdSense Coaching Club

Edmond, OK (PRWEB) May 9, 2006—With Internet publishers looking for ways to monetize their sites, Google has become one of the most revered sites due to its contextual advertising program, Google AdSense. This text-based ad service is generating four-, five-, and six-figure incomes for many web site owners. With this increased interest in this revolutionary revenue-generating program, site owners are looking for ways to increase their AdSense income further.

Today, Joel Comm announced the launch of his Premier AdSense Coaching Club, an exclusive member site designed to help Internet web site owners make more money with the AdSense program. Joel Comm is the Internet's recognized Google AdSense expert, and as author of the Web's best-selling AdSense e-book, "What Google Never Told You About Making Money with AdSense" (now in its third edition), Joel is distinctly qualified to teach others how to multiply their AdSense revenue.

"Once you understand the basics of making more money with AdSense, you can instantly begin seeing an increase to your revenue stream," says Joel Comm. "But many people are leaving a lot of money on the table by not taking advanced steps to increase revenue. My exclusive coaching club is designed for people who are serious about taking their AdSense and overall site revenue to the next level."

Joel's Premier AdSense Coaching Club contains many features, all of which are instantly accessible to members around the clock. Features include:

(Continued)

(Continued)

♦ How-To Videos—Narrated by Joel, these videos visually demonstrate strategies for increasing revenue designed for everyone from novice to advanced site publishers. Spotlighted this month are the Blogging and AdSense 101 videos, featuring 30 minutes of easy-to-follow instructions that can get anyone started with content creation and the Google AdSense program within minutes.

♦ A monthly two-hour telecourse featuring interviews with leading industry experts that are guaranteed to present new opportunities for maximizing AdSense revenue. Past guests have included PR Secrets Expert Marc Harty, and Jeff Walker, the recognized Product Launch guru.

♦ A monthly members-only special report revealing Joel's latest strategies for creating wealth online. Current reports include the 30-page instantly downloadable documents, "Getting Started with AdSense and Blogging" and "The Yahoo! Publishing Network Quickstart Guide."

♦ Privileged access to Joel's AdSense Mastermind Group, including opportunities to network with other Premium members and develop joint ventures.

♦ Real-life case studies, featuring video examples with Joel's narration. These real-life site critiques demonstrate strategies which can be immediately implemented on any web site.

♦ Additional bonuses and surprises for Premier Members!

The Premier AdSense Coaching Club is the result of high demand from Joel's readers and is accessed online for a low monthly fee at www.joelcomm.com/coachingclub.html.

(Continued)

(*Continued*)

"I am thrilled to provide a wealth of training information and resources to my premier members," says Comm. "With over 1,000 members currently in the coaching club, many have stopped leaving money on the table and are now enjoying more in their bank accounts!"

About Joel Comm

Joel Comm is an author, technology buff, and entrepreneur who has been successfully marketing products and services online since 1995. He is the founder of InfoMedia, Inc., a company that strives to provide family-friendly entertainment and other useful resources through web sites that include DealofDay.com, WorldVillage.com, FamilyFirst.com, and FreeBitz.com. Joel is the author of many books focused on teaching people how to make money online and is frequently invited to speak and teach at conferences and seminars. For interviews or more information, contact InfoMedia, Inc., at (405) 348-2800, or visit www.JoelComm.com.

You can see how this release contains all the elements that a press release should possess. There's the headline, the quote, a bullet list, a quote at the end to round things off, and a short bio that tells reporters who I am.

But this isn't a media story. I don't expect my local newspaper to pick up this story and run with it. The newspaper's readers don't care that I've just launched an AdSense Coaching Club. None of them know who I am, and many of them won't know about AdSense.

The only outlets that are going to pick up a press release like this are those that already know me and understand AdSense. It's a story aimed at a core audience—an audience of Internet marketers who are most likely to become customers. While it's unlikely to appear in a mainstream newspaper, it will be picked up by blogs and web sites that discuss AdSense and Internet marketing. I won't get a great deal of expert branding, but I should get some sales.

Compare that press release to the one on the next page.

Google AdSense Guru's Breakfast Up for Bid at eBay

Edmond, OK (PRWEB) June 8, 2006—No one wants to buy a half-eaten breakfast on eBay . . . unless that half-eaten breakfast belongs to a celebrity who is offering 30 minutes of one-on-one personal consulting for the lucky winner of the leftovers! That's precisely what one attendee of Carl Galletti's Internet Marketing Superconference decided to pursue when Google AdSense expert Joel Comm took the stage on Saturday, June 3, in Las Vegas, Nevada!

Comm, known for his Amazon.com #1 best-selling book *The AdSense Code,* took the platform and offered anyone in the audience the opportunity to share his breakfast. Lin Ennis, sitting in the front row, seized the opportunity to enjoy the other half of Joel's bagel with egg and bacon and roasted potatoes. Little did Comm know that his breakfast sandwich would appear on eBay.com, the world's largest auction site, in the form of an auction!

"When I saw my breakfast was up for auction, I thought I would offer the winner the same thing they would receive if they actually sat down to enjoy the breakfast with me," says Joel Comm. "So the winner of the auction will also receive a free 30-minute telephone consultation providing the opportunity to discuss my best Internet moneymaking strategies."

Ennis, a resident of Sedona, Arizona, has vowed to donate all proceeds from the breakfast auction to the "Young Internet Entrepreneurs of Sedona." She has also included an additional set of bonuses that would appeal to anyone wanting to learn how to make money online.

Joel Comm's breakfast auction is set to end on June 13, 2006, at 11 a.m. To view the breakfast and bid in this auction, go to www.adsense-secrets.com/breakfast.html.

To read more about Joel Comm or his Amazon.com #1 best seller *The AdSense Code,* go to www.joelcomm.com.

(Continued)

(Continued)

About Joel Comm

Joel Comm is an author, technology buff, and entrepreneur who has been successfully marketing products and services online since 1995. He is the founder of InfoMedia, Inc., a company that strives to provide family-friendly entertainment and other useful resources through web sites that include www.DealofDay.com, www.WorldVillage.com, and www.FamilyFirst.com. Joel is the cofounder of Yahoo! Games and the author of many books focused on teaching people how to make money online. He is frequently invited to speak and teach at conferences and seminars. For interviews or more information, contact InfoMedia, Inc. at (405) 348-2800, or visit www.JoelComm.com.

This is a press release aimed at a much more general audience. It's entertaining rather than sales-y, and it could be picked up by anyone. Any publication looking for a funny story would be interested in running it. It touches on the Internet, on the range of goods available on eBay . . . and it's ridiculous.

Although it's meant to be funny, look at how I'm portrayed in the press release. I still come across as an expert. The press release describes me as an author, a speaker, and someone whom people will bid for in order to win half an hour's coaching. It's a light, attention-grabbing story. But the impression is serious.

It's a different way of writing press releases. The format remains the same. There are quotes that show reporters they'll be getting usable sound bites. There's still a headline, and I still include a bio at the end so that reporters know whom they'll be talking to. But the subject is meant to appeal to anyone, not just to people who already know me or my subject. That will spread my name even further—and help with my branding.

You can use both of these kinds of press releases. Whenever you want to win publicity, you can write one press release that's filled with basic information for the blogs and web sites in your field. And you can write a more general release—one that's entertaining, informative, or fun—pitched to a wider audience. If you get both releases right, you could pick up publicity in both channels.

Distributing the press releases has changed, too. Once you had to program a long list of numbers into a fax machine. Then you could use a computer-based fax program to do the same thing. Many reporters still like to receive their press releases by fax, but it's perfectly appropriate to send e-mails to them if you have their details—or use a distribution service. I like PRWeb

Figure 7.3   This is speaking.joelcomm.com, the web site that I use to promote my public speaking work. Note how I use my press appearances to build my branding and reinforce the impression of expertise. If *Fortune*, CNN, and *BusinessWeek* want to speak to me, then I must know what I'm talking about, right? Once you've won publicity a few times with press releases, you might well find that the media view you as a trusted source and come back to you regularly.

(www.prweb.com) and Expert Click (www.ExpertClick.com). PRWeb prices start around $80 per press release, but Expert Click allows you to send 52 releases for approximately $800. Both can be very effective, and they are easy to use.

You should be using press releases as part of your business strategy. The more often you appear in the media, the more you'll drive home the idea that you're an expert. You'll be able to add the logo of the outlet to your web site, thus building your credibility. Other reporters will see that you've been interviewed, know who you are, and feel easier about contacting you for interviews.

Whenever you bring out a new product, you should send out a press release. Whenever you launch a new coaching workshop, you should send out a press release. Whenever you do anything, you should send out a press release and use that opportunity to build your brand as an expert across a wide audience (Figure 7.3).

Getting Started: Low-End Coaching

When you see a well-known speaker take to the stage, it's easy to feel that you'll never be doing that. You might not. Not everyone feels comfortable sharing their knowledge on the stage. But if it is something you want to do, then it is something you *can* do. Coaches—even the biggest names—aren't superhuman individuals capable of leaping a 50-foot stage in a single bound. They're just regular entrepreneurs—like you—who have built up their knowledge and want to share it. They've managed to build their brand and spread it to such an extent that they're now invited to address conferences, put on workshops, and guide other entrepreneurs toward their dreams. They sell coaching kits that cost thousands of dollars, and when it comes to personal consulting, the sky's the limit.

Yet none of them started out that way. All of the biggest coaches you can think of started small, teaching their skills to small groups of people who were keen to learn.

It's a process that relies on your own skills and your own effort. You won't need to depend on receiving an invitation from a conference organizer, and you won't be left hoping that people will turn up so that you won't be addressing an empty room.

Organizing your own coaching events and selling your own consulting services might be hard work. It might even involve a little financial risk (although it doesn't have to). But the immediate returns can be enormous, and it's the best way to get your feet wet and build experience. You don't want your very first coaching session to be with someone who has paid a giant sum for the privilege of being a guinea pig. After all, your coaching fees won't just reflect the value of your knowledge; they'll also reflect the ease with which you transfer that knowledge to your clients.

A low-end coaching program—the kind best suited to someone just starting out as a coach—can consist of a number of different packages. The most basic is telephone coaching. The meat of the package will be a number of monthly telephone calls. These can last anywhere from half an hour to an hour and might take place once a week or three times a month. You can also toss in a few valuable information products, such as an e-book laying out your ideas, a free assessment of where the business stands at the moment, and a personalized action plan that can act as a guide for the client's development over the course of the program. You might also want to make yourself available for e-mail correspondence in between phone calls.

The rate for a program like that could easily be around $400 to $500 a month, with a six-month minimum commitment. Considering that the total amount of time actually spent working with the client might be only an hour on the phone, an hour preparing for the call, and the odd 10 minutes here and there to write an e-mail, it's easy to see that even this simple formula can deliver great hourly rates.

You wouldn't need more than half a dozen telephone clients a month to give your income a meaningful boost and your business a loud KaChing.

Alternatively, or additionally, you could offer coaching in person. This would also provide the assessment, action plan, and any other information products you want to toss in, but mostly it would consist of meetings at the client's office once a week or several times a month. The meetings would last longer than the telephone calls and allow you to interact with the client a little better. Fees for this kind of coaching are often three times that of telephone consultations. They have to take into account the time spent traveling to and from the client's office as well as the extra value of having you on the premises.

Of course, personal coaching will usually be limited to people within your catchment area. As you grow your coaching business, you might well find that you're getting requests from people farther away who will be willing to pay your travel expenses and even your hotel fees. When you're putting in that much effort to coach someone, your fees will need to reflect the work involved. Considering the long flights and time spent away from home, you should charge enough to feel grateful when prospective clients either say no or agree to your terms.

Those are the two most basic models for coaching, but you can also break out segments of your coaching to create niche products. Business coach Suzanne Muusers, for example, offers marketing consulting services and web site and SEO consultations from her site ProsperityCoaching.biz (www.prosperitycoaching.biz). These allow her to provide focused, personalized knowledge that solves one specific problem at a time for a client.

It's possible to market coaching in a number of different ways. As you launch a new program, you should certainly be writing a press release, and you should also write a press release when one of your clients reaches his or her goals. There's nothing the media like more than a success story, especially if it contains lessons their readers can use, too. That's always going to be valuable branding for you.

Your web site will be helpful too, and if you link your coaching site to your main blog or web site, you should find that you receive a steady flow of readers who pass from that site and want your advice in person.

Another option though is to put on miniworkshops. This can be a great way to make yourself known to people in your area who might be willing to sign up as personal clients. Entry to the workshop would be free. The content would contain an introduction to your topic and a few tips that people can take away with them. Pitch it as a lecture on "Turning Your Knitting Hobby into a Business" from a professional knitting expert or a talk on "Why Start-Ups Fail" from an experienced entrepreneur; make it clear that you're not selling or charging, and you should find that you can even pick up free space in libraries and community centers.

Some of the people who attend may become clients. Others may choose to order the information products that you make available at the back of the room. Either way, you get a chance to put your name in front of a targeted audience for little cost. You can even use that lecture as an introduction to a group course. This won't be as personalized as one-on-one coaching, but if you keep the group small and emphasize that spaces are limited, you'll create a sense of urgency that's more likely to have people signing up.

It's even possible to run these group sessions online and at a distance, giving you more opportunities for marketing. Dr. Gina J. Hiatt (www.academicladder.com), for example, is a dissertation and tenure coach who helps students write their theses and academics boost their careers. She provides a range of different coaching environments, including an Academic Writing Club, which is a four-week online course; individual coaching, consisting of 30- to 45-minute telephone sessions; and group coaching, made up of a 60-minute group telephone call and dedicated listserv. Software programs like Group Coaching Manager (www.groupcoachingmanager.com) make managing group coaching relatively simple.

Of course, it's also possible to sell coaching products such as online courses and DVDs. These won't be personalized in the way that one-on-one or group coaching can be, but they should form part of your coaching revenue streams.

A basic coaching program is fairly easy to create. The packages themselves follow a familiar formula, and the fees can be very high, offering hourly rates of at least three, and sometimes four, figures—that's a seriously loud KaChing. Your success will depend mainly on your ability to build your name as an expert and to instill confidence in potential students to sign up to receive your knowledge.

You should find that's something that will happen naturally as you create good content and build your community.

Kicking It Up: High-End Coaching

But what do you do then? You have a number of clients whom you speak with on the phone once a week. You do a weekly group session using conference calls so that everyone can learn from everyone else's experience. And you might even have the odd local client whom you're teaching on an individual, in-person basis.

In addition, you're still writing your web site content, earning from ads, and pitching your information products.

All of those things are going to deliver steady streams of cash, and if they're done right, they're going to deliver that cash in amounts that will surprise you. You'll be hearing KaChing rings all around you, and they'll be so loud you'll think you're working in a bell tower.

But it's not enough.

The real benefit of putting information online and making it available to others isn't the money it will bring you. That's wonderful, life-changing stuff but it's not the biggest reward.

The real thrill comes when you see other people taking that information, putting it to work, and seeing success themselves. I know that sounds a bit cheesy, and it wasn't my main motivation when I started online marketing. I wanted to make money. But once I'd made money, and once I saw that money continued to come in regularly and abundantly, I really did start to get the biggest kick out of sharing my knowledge and seeing other people enjoy success.

All of the strategies I've described so far will help you do that to some extent. But nothing will do it as efficiently as a high-end coaching program.

This is a step up from other coaching programs. Low-end coaching programs will let you provide personalized solutions to others, who will then have to take those solutions and implement them themselves. You tell them what they have to do, and you have to hope they'll do it.

Many will, but plenty won't. Even after paying for their coaching program, they'll listen to you and nod and thank you, but when it comes to rolling up their sleeves and battling the problems involved in creating a business, they won't bother. Instead, they'll sign up for someone else's coaching program and wonder why they aren't achieving the success they expect. You're being paid, so you're happy, but if they aren't willing to put in the work, then they won't be happy, and that's always going to be a problem.

High-end coaching is about results. It means helping people who are genuinely serious about achieving success and giving them the knowledge and the tools they need to achieve it themselves. It also means being selective about the people you coach.

This isn't an attempt to sell as many items as possible to as many people as possible. Your information products should do that. This is about choosing the people you want to guide toward their goals so that you can have the satisfaction of seeing them succeed.

There's something in it for you too, of course. When a person you've mentored is able to say that he or she became a millionaire because of your advice and guidance, the perception of your expertise goes through the roof. Your sales will rise, your web sites will receive more attention, and you'll have people lining up to join your coaching programs.

Because you're being selective, and because you're prepared to give more to your students—more time, more attention, more of a guarantee even (it's not unusual for top-end coaching programs to promise an ROI of perhaps "$5,000 or your money back")—you get to charge a giant amount of money.

You can be really bold here and base the fee on the actual returns you think that the students will see. That's not the amount they *might* see if they bothered to implement your ideas. It's the amount they *will* see when they do.

Sure, a high price will put people off. You *want* to put those people off. You want to coach only those people who have the confidence, drive, and energy to succeed. They don't expect you to do it for them. They expect you to tell them what they need to do so that they can go out and do it themselves. They really will understand that spending $5,000 (or whatever it is you're charging) is going to be a great investment.

There are a couple of models for this kind of high-end coaching.

The first is an enlarged and selective version of your regular telephone-based coaching programs. The spaces are limited; you choose only applicants you want to work with; and there's more contact each week.

This was the approach taken by John Taylor (www.johntaylorsblog.com), a marketing consultant and publisher. John has produced several information products and is active on WarriorForum (www.warriorforum.com), a meeting place for Internet marketers. He used the forum to announce a special coaching program about Internet marketing. The spaces were limited, the fee was $697, and in return, he would provide two 30-minute Skype calls each week and answer up to five questions per day by e-mail.

To be accepted into the program, applicants had to jump through a bunch of hoops, which included stating the amount of time and money they were prepared to invest in their success each week, describing the objectives they wanted to reach, and writing a 200-word article on their best Internet marketing achievement so far (Figure 7.4).

This isn't a coaching program aimed at just anyone, and John isn't trying to make as many sales as possible. He's advertising his coaching on a site where he knows he'll find dedicated students, and he's weeding out anyone who isn't completely serious about achieving success.

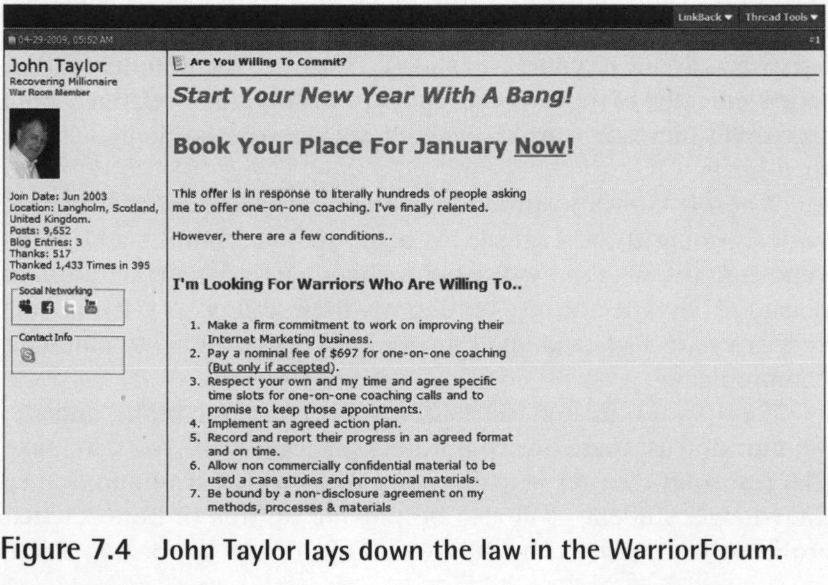

Figure 7.4 John Taylor lays down the law in the WarriorForum.

But the format of the coaching is still very simple. The students themselves won't need to do more than take part in a Skype chat twice a week, and John can remain in his office in Scotland, talking to students around the world.

The second model is to make your coaching more intensive. Instead of working with someone over a period of a month—or several months if you want to renew the coaching program—you cram the entire program into one packed weekend.

For that period, you're going to be completely dedicated. It will be a little like organizing your own miniconference, so students are going to need room and board as well as instruction. You might well spend more time preparing for the program than you'll actually spend conducting it.

However, the returns can be enormous. Paul Hartunian, a professional speaker and publicity expert, used to train other potential speakers to create a career for themselves on the lecture circuit. His three-day workshops took place at his ranch in New Jersey and cost $4,995. Classes were limited to just 15 students at a time, which meant that three days of coaching would bring him as much as $74,925.

Clearly, only a small fraction of the community you build through your blog, your information products, and your social media networking will be interested in paying a four-figure fee and spending a few days at one of your workshops. Those are the people who are most dedicated to their success though, so charging a relatively high price will increase your chances of seeing your students achieve their goals.

When it comes to promoting this kind of coaching program, value is going to be critical. Even the most ambitious and confident students will think twice before handing over several thousand dollars. They are not just betting on their ability to achieve success; they are also gambling on your knowledge and your ability to communicate.

There is no greater test of the power of your brand and the amount of trust that your community places in you. You can make that test a little easier to pass by making clear that in addition to knowledge, students will also be picking up lots of bonuses that are worth at least as much as the cost of the workshop itself.

Paul Hartunian, for example, places the bios of speakers who have passed through his workshop on his web site at www.hartunian .com/speakers, thus giving them some valuable advertising. He also supplies the actual contract he uses when taking bookings, allowing students to adapt it for their own businesses. That costs him nothing, but saves his students a small fortune in legal fees.

These kinds of workshops aren't likely to be regular events. The high costs ensure that they will appeal to only a tiny fraction of your community, which means that finding new leads could take awhile. But at these prices, they don't need to be regular events. You'd have to do only one or two a year to give your income a very loud, extra KaChing.

Case Studies

You're not the first person to want to make money online. That's good news. The pioneers had a lot of work to do. They had to figure out which tools worked the best, how to use them, and what sort of content they needed to serve in order to build audiences that they could monetize. They had to decide how to build the web sites, lay out the ads, and format the articles. They had to create the Internet that we take for granted today.

It was a process that took time, lots of experiments, and plenty of failures. Occasionally, as you're surfing the Web, you'll come across an old-style web site, complete with flashing horizontal lines, cheesy animations, and cursor trails, and you'll wonder how on earth a site like that ever managed to attract visitors. The answer is that there wasn't much else on the Web at the time.

Now that there is a *lot* more on the Web, those sites aren't making money. The sites that are making money are the ones that follow the formulas that work.

In this chapter, I describe a number of web sites that make great models for entrepreneurs. Now I don't know whether these sites are making a lot of money. I know that some are making some money; I suspect that others are making giant piles of money; and it's likely that still others could be making a lot of money if they really wanted to. But perhaps that's not the main reason they were created. How much these sites are actually making isn't important. What *is* important is how much *you* could be making if you follow the models shown on these pages.

Content Sites

All web sites rely on good content. That's true whether their goal is simply to attract readers and have fun or to make money for the site's publisher. In this section, I look at a number of sites that offer great content and surround that content with a range of different types of revenue channels.

TRAVELS WITH SHEILA

I'm going to start these case studies with a site I know well. TravelsWithSheila.com (www.travelswithsheila.com) is my mom's web site (Figure 8.1). It's also a great example of how anyone—and I really do mean *anyone*—can create multiple revenue streams online based on the knowledge that they've built up indulging their passion.

My mom is nuts about travel. She's been everywhere, and she's always on the move. I don't think there's a country she hasn't been to, an airline she hasn't flown, or some personal belonging she hasn't left in a hotel room somewhere. During those travels, she's built up a huge bank of knowledge. She can tell you how to find archaeological digs in Israel, trek safely in Kashmir, and feed the penguins in Patagonia. She can also tell you which travel companies have the best bargains, how to pack smartly, and why "dynamic conversion" always costs you more when picking up the bill in a foreign restaurant. When it comes to travel, she's a gold mine of information.

When it comes to computers though, she's never really been ahead of the curve. It took me quite a while to persuade her that sharing her travel knowledge and stories online could generate enough money to help pay for those constant round-the-world trips. Since launching TravelsWithSheila.com, she's come to appreciate that all the time I spent playing with the computer when I should have

Figure 8.1   Home page of my mom's site TravelsWithSheila.com. Note how the first thing that hits you is the AdSense ads. That's smart positioning! She also has a search box and a newsletter field for capturing e-mail addresses, all above the fold.

been doing my homework actually gave me a great education. That's priceless.

The first thing that strikes you when you reach the site is two AdSense units. They dominate the above-the-fold content area. In fact, of the real content, you can see only the headline and a few lines of the first article beneath those AdSense units. The pictures running down the side of the page, which look like vacation snapshots, help to frame those ads so that they blend into the page, but it's the ads that are front and center. This site is designed to make money (Figure 8.2).

There are more AdSense units in the articles themselves. Each page has a horizontal text unit immediately below the headline, a placement that makes the ads look like navigation links. Another square unit is embedded right at the beginning of the article, and

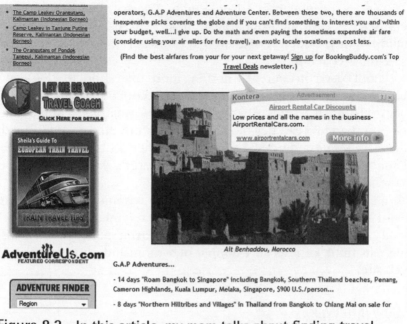

Figure 8.2   In this article, my mom talks about finding travel bargains, and she works an affiliate link into the text. You can also see a Kontera ad, a link to her telephone coaching, her train guide information product, and the adventure finder widget that pays on an affiliate basis. It's good content packed with subtle, moneymaking channels.

there's usually another one at the end to catch readers once they've finished reading and before they click away.

But AdSense isn't the only method that the site uses to monetize readers. The text also contains Kontera ads, and in the left column there's an interactive tool that lets readers find quotes for their next adventure vacation. That's an affiliate widget. Above it is a link to an information product, a 17-page guide that my mom wrote about European train travel. Readers can download it for seven bucks. And above that is a small ad that links to my mom's travel coaching service. For $47, she's available for half-hour phone consultations. (Buyers also receive the e-book and a subscription to her weekly newsletter.)

There's revenue from AdSense units. There's revenue from Kontera. There's revenue from affiliate links. There's revenue from an information product. And there's revenue from some simple and occasional coaching.

It's all based on content—nothing more than short articles—and the specific knowledge that those articles contain. That's vital. My mom tells great stories. She has lots of information to share, and the people who read her blog are both entertained and informed. AdSense, Kontera, her e-book, and the other tools that she places on her site give my mom a number of different ways to cash in on those stories and her expertise.

It's all very simple. There's nothing technically challenging about the site—my mom really isn't the technical type. It's just good content monetized with the Web's proven monetization tools. You can think of it as an example of a mom-and-pop commercial web site.

READWRITEWEB

TravelsWithSheila.com is a one-person web site that uses good content and a variety of channels to turn the information in that content into cash. It also uses information gathered by doing something fun. My mom doesn't get paid to travel—except when talking about it online.

ReadWriteWeb.com (www.readwriteweb.com) provides a very different model (Figure 8.3). Created in 2003, the site is a technology blog rated by Technorati (a search engine for blogs) as one of the top 20 blogs on the Web. It was created by Richard MacManus, a New Zealander who had previously worked as an analyst and researcher in Silicon Valley. The site made use of the knowledge that he had built up while working with technology firms.

Today, it's no longer a one-person site. Although Richard continues to contribute regularly, the site has a long list of staff writers and guest writers, as well as a production editor, marketing and experience manager, and other people with big job titles. It's not just a blog; it's a business with a full-time staff.

It's no surprise that ReadWriteWeb uses a variety of methods to monetize its content and ensure that those staff members are paid.

Figure 8.3   ReadWriteWeb is a giant publishing company of a site, with multiple contributors, premium reports ... and many sponsors.

One of those channels is syndication. The *New York Times* technology section buys the site's content. That's not something you can rely on, although it's certainly great when it happens. Advertising though is something you can rely on when you're producing good content, and ReadWriteWeb uses a number of different methods. There's a vertical AdSense unit in the right column, which is always going to be helpful, but it appears that most of the advertising space on the site is sold directly as sponsored ads. The ads appear as graphic squares of 125 × 125 pixels that appear on a monthly basis on the side of every page. Companies can place those ads by contacting ReadWriteWeb directly. The site also runs CPM ads, which are managed by Federated Media (www.federatedmedia.net), a web site advertising agency.

The fees for those kinds of ads vary. A 125 × 125 pixel text ad costs $91 for a week's placement. A 300 × 250 graphic ad costs $1,560 for 60,000 impressions, the minimum number that Federated Media will sell.

In addition, the site also offers a number of reports. These are carefully researched information products that include profiles, stats, and case studies. The prices start at $300.

If all of that isn't enough, ReadWriteWeb has also created a number of separate channels, including ReadWriteEnterprise for businesses and ReadWriteStart, which profiles start-ups and entrepreneurs and is sponsored by Microsoft. They're both accessible from ReadWriteWeb's main site and show one way in which it's possible to expand a successful site into new areas and still cash in on its brand.

ReadWriteWeb started small, as a way for a professional technology expert to share his expertise with a wider audience, but it's now grown into a publishing company in its own right. It's still run by Richard MacManus from his home office in the New Zealand town of Lower Hutt.

ORIGAMI BLOG

So far, we've seen how it's possible to turn a passion into a profitable online business venture. We've also seen just what can happen when you put your business knowledge on the Web and use the tools available to monetize it: You can end up running a successful, specialized publishing company.

But what happens if your passion *is* your profession?

First, you've already hit the jackpot. There aren't many people who are lucky enough to make a living doing the things they love to do. If you're one of them, then you're in select company—and the Web can help you squeeze even more revenue out of your pastime.

Cindy Ng has a degree in business economics, but her real enthusiasm is for paper folding. She designs origami kits and has crafted origami-inspired jewelry that is sold in a number of museums, including the San Francisco Museum of Modern Art, the Art

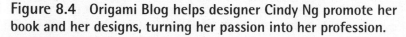

Figure 8.4 Origami Blog helps designer Cindy Ng promote her book and her designs, turning her passion into her profession.

Institute of Chicago, the Smithsonian, and London's Victoria and Albert Museum. She's also the author of *Girligami*, a series of origami models designed to appeal to women (Figure 8.4).

Origami Blog (www.origamiblog.com) is just one of Cindy's web sites, but it acts as a main entry point, attracting people interested in the topic and then sending them out to other sites where they can buy her products. There's no third-party advertising on the site. That's a missed opportunity. Blended into the content, there's no reason that AdSense units, for example, would put off readers or look out of place. Instead, at the top of the page, Cindy places links to her "shop," Origami Bijou (www.origamibijou.com); her book, *Girligami* (www.girligami.com); and her online store at Etsy, a craft site where people can buy her origami kits. She also links to her social media pages on Facebook and Twitter, which helps her to build a community around her interest and her designs.

This is a different way of monetizing information compared to the examples we've seen before. Cindy's goal isn't to earn income from views of the content she posts but to position herself as an expert on origami and to earn direct income by selling products. It's a method of using specialized content—in this case, content that's both a hobby and a profession—to build an audience and guide that audience to places where they can make purchases.

Affiliate-Supported Sites

The content-rich sites we've looked at so far use a number of different methods to turn information into cash. Sometimes they've included affiliate links as one of those revenue channels. When TravelsWithSheila.com discussed cheap ways to travel, for example, the article included an affiliate link to a recommended travel service. But affiliate links aren't always appropriate on every page. Sales usually rely on recommendations for specific products, so if you're not discussing a product, then an affiliate link will often bring limited results.

On the other hand, that does mean that sites that focus on products can really cash in with affiliate relationships. In this section, I describe how a couple of sites use affiliate products in two very different ways.

TELESCOPE REVIEWS

Telescope Reviews (www.telescopereviews.org.uk) is exactly what you might expect of a site optimized to make money from affiliate products. Based in the United Kingdom, the site offers "unbiased reviews" of a wide range of telescope brands. But you have to look for those reviews. Surf to the home page, and the first thing you'll see is three navigation tabs leading to "home," "cheap telescopes," and "cheap binoculars." To find links leading to reviews of different brands or models, readers have to scroll past the ads. This is a site in which selling, and leading people to buy, comes before the content.

Beneath those tabs is a long list of Amazon affiliate links. To the right, an Amazon widget allows the site another opportunity to earn from an affiliate sale. You have to scroll about half a dozen screens before you see the end of the affiliate list and reach the first review.

What the site calls "unbiased" actually means impersonal. There are no accounts of the writer using the telescope, what he or she finds interesting about it, or why it marks a development in home-based astronomy or the science of peeking at neighbors. Instead, readers receive a long, detailed list of features . . . followed by a box filled with affiliate links.

There are a lot of sites like this on the Web. Publishers know that buyers research major purchases online before parting with their cash, so creating a review site looks like an easy way to earn a commission on those sales. But while it's possible to make some money surrounding related words with affiliate ads, to make *real* money—the kind of money that makes the whole thing worthwhile—the content still has to be good.

The content on Telescope Reviews isn't good. It looks like it was thrown together by a five-buck-an-article content writer in Bangalore. It's unlikely that anyone seriously interested in buying a telescope is going to hang around long enough to decide to buy, and they certainly won't come back. Whatever the publisher is saving on writing expenses will go to pay for search engine optimization and traffic generation to keep people flowing through.

It's much easier to produce good content about products related to a topic that interests you. Use that content to create a community, build trust, and bring readers back, and you're much more likely to see them clicking through your affiliate links and sending you money.

DigsDigs

If Telescope Reviews is a good example of how *not* to create an affiliate site, DigsDigs (www.digsdigs.com) is an excellent example of the right way to make the most of the opportunities provided by affiliates (Figure 8.5).

The site offers information about home decorating and interior design, a field rich in potential affiliate sales. But it doesn't rely on affiliate sales and it doesn't shove affiliate links forward at the expense of good content. Instead, the site offers the kind of content that creates desire and provides a way for readers to satisfy that desire by making a purchase.

That also means making the most of other revenue streams. Telescope Reviews places an AdSense half banner above each

Figure 8.5   DigsDigs writes about products, but offers much more than reviews, recommendations, and affiliate links.

article, but the units are not well optimized and are easily ignored. DigsDigs uses a horizontal link unit directly beneath the navigation bar and has changed the color of the links to match the color of the site's own links and headlines: an attractive purple (Figure 8.6). That's smart blending. The ads now look like content. There's an image ad on the right, and more square units can be found above each article and sometimes between the images contained within articles, a placement that's close to impossible to miss.

The result is lots of ads about a range of different household topics, but they aren't obtrusive and they don't feel like they're being pushed on the reader. That's certainly true of the affiliate links. These don't appear in every article, even when the post is discussing a product.

That makes for some smart choices. DigsDigs talks about products as wide-ranging as designer bathtubs and elite coffeemakers. Many of those products are going to be interesting but produce few sales. Others are fun and practical and cheap enough to be an impulse buy. If it's commercial enough to be on Amazon, there's a chance that a reader will be interested enough to snap it up. That's when DigsDigs tends to include affiliate links.

LIFTING HUMAN CD HOLDER

This is the first of 3 nice Wrapables products. It measures 4.7" x 9.5" x 8.25" and holds 10 CDs just for 40$. You can buy it here.

Figure 8.6   DigsDigs is a great example of the right way to do an affiliate site.

The site produces content that's interesting and attractive. It's designed in a way that makes it a pleasant read, with pictures that allow for quick browsing and fun viewing. It also has a Twitter timeline that enables it to build the base of a community, members of which are likely to click through the links and make money for the publisher.

DigsDigs isn't *obviously* a product site. But when it discusses products, it's already built up enough trust and interest to have a good chance of turning those mentions into affiliate sales.

Information Products

Information products come in a range of different forms and play a range of different roles in the Internet businesses of entrepreneurs. For some publishers, they might provide nothing more than a little supplementary income, an extra revenue source on a site that makes most of its KaChing from advertising. For others, they're the main deal. The web site helps to promote those products and build a brand.

BRAD CALLEN

Brad Callen might not be long out of his twenties, but there's little he doesn't know about Internet marketing. He has his own software company, Bryxen Software, and he's produced a series of information products about a variety of different aspects of online marketing. If you visit his site, BradCallen.com (www.bradcallen.com), you'll see that the entire first screen is taken up with plugs for one of his products and notifications of two others that are in production (Figure 8.7). Choose to ignore those ads—and that's not easy to do—and when you scroll down the page, you'll see a list of testimonials, then some solid blog content packed with great information. The first item in the navigation bar leads to products, not content. Brad is focused on selling goods, either software products or information products.

The differences between those information products are interesting, too. *SEO Mindset* is a physical book delivered by mail. It's also free. Instead of generating a KaChing from the cover price, Brad uses the book to lead buyers into his search engine optimization

Figure 8.7   On Brad Callen's web site, information products come first.

membership site. Readers get a month's free membership but must then pay a monthly fee of $39. They can cancel at any time, even before they've made a single payment, but Brad is confident that having tried it for a month, most will stick around.

His information product then becomes an incentive for an even more lucrative revenue channel.

That's not true of his other products. *Press Release Fire* is a traditional e-book that sells for $19.95 and is promoted through a hard-hitting traditional sales page. You can see it at www. pressreleasefire.com.

Elite Sessions consists of 90-minute audio interviews, complete with PDF transcripts, with 11 leading marketers. The discs sell for $147. There was no writing involved here. Brad just sat and talked with a bunch of other experts about a topic that they all know and understand. There's no easier way to turn information into KaChing.

The only ads on Brad's site are for his own products. There are no AdSense units and no affiliate links. Instead, his blog posts show off his expertise, enabling him to create a brand strong enough to encourage people to pay for his information, especially after they've been persuaded by a powerful sales letter.

BLOOM BIKE SHOP

Brad Callen uses information products as a way of creating large amounts of passive revenue. But that's not the only way to use information products. You can also produce something very simple and, instead of selling it, use it as a way to market your site, build your brand, and create your e-mail list.

That's what BloomBikeShop.com (www.bloombikeshop.com) does. The site provides useful information about bicycle repair and maintenance, including tutorials and articles. It monetizes those articles with AdSense units above and below the posts, with CPM banner ads, with affiliate links in genuinely informative product reviews, and with links to shopping sites (Figure 8.8).

It also offers a free e-book to anyone who agrees to register for the site's e-mail newsletter. That allows the site to keep a list of its visitors and to send deals and offers to anyone who has visited the site in the past, even if they haven't come back.

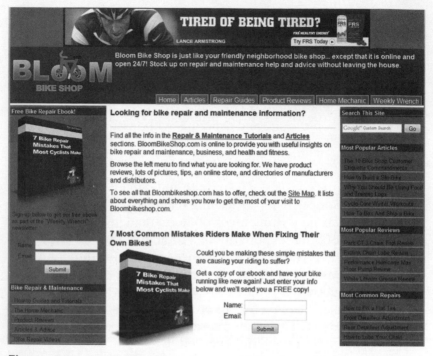

Figure 8.8   BloomBikeShop.com provides a ton of information about bicycle maintenance ... and uses an information product to capture e-mail addresses. Couldn't be simpler!

The e-book itself is nothing grand. Called *7 Common Bike Repair Mistakes That Most Riders Make,* it lists a number of myths that bike owners believe when they try to repair their own bicycles. With little more than 1,000 words of content, it could easily have been put on the site and made available as Web content like all the other articles. Instead, publisher Levi Bloom has turned it into a PDF document and placed it behind a registration barrier. If you enter your e-mail address, you'll receive a double-opt-in confirmation message from AWeber. When you confirm your address, you'll be given a link to a page that lets you read the PDF file.

It's very easy, couldn't have taken more than a few minutes to put together, and it's likely to have had a massive effect on the value of the site's e-mail list.

Subscription Sites

Subscription sites are often relatively complex. They aren't necessarily difficult to build; the tools available now mean that you have to put in some effort, but you don't need a degree in computer science or a giant sack of cash to pay a programmer.

What you will need is a community of knowledgeable people who are active on the site and generous with their advice. You also need to be willing to put in the effort to keep the conversations ticking and ensure that the site continues to deliver value for the subscription fee. That can involve anything from starting your own discussion streams to getting rid of people who are rude to other contributors. Subscription fees usually keep out the worst types, but you do want to keep your site a pleasant, helpful place for everyone.

WEBMASTERWORLD

My own subscription site is pretty complex. I've packed in a ton of features in my aim to overdeliver. But a subscription site doesn't have to be that complicated. WebMasterWorld (www.webmasterworld .com) is essentially a forum, and for a long time, it was a free forum (Figure 8.9). When it came to monetizing the site, there was a problem: A forum is a place for open discussion, and those open discussions often involve criticisms of the companies advertising on the site.

Rather than attempt to censor discussions, WebMasterWorld instead chose to ask members to pay a subscription fee of $89 for six months or $149 for a year. The hope was that the value of the sometimes technical information on offer would more than pay for the cost of the subscription.

Some of the older threads can be read for free. They act as sources of information, inviting potential participants in and demonstrating the quality of the knowledge on offer. But to start a thread or to take part in one, users have to sign up.

There are a couple of points to note here.

The first is WebMasterWorld's simplicity. There are no whiz-bang features. Subscribers are paying for the chance to access each

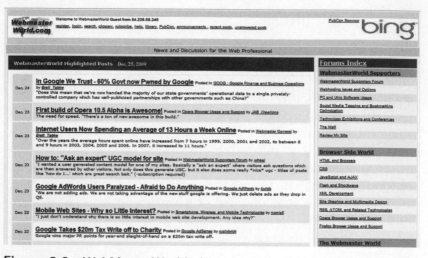

Figure 8.9   WebMasterWorld gives some content away for free. The rest you have to pay for.

other's knowledge. That's all. The site provides a means for them to do that.

The second point is that WebMasterWorld depends on its users not just to pay the subscription fees, but also to deliver value for those fees. The site was free for a long time and built up a solid reputation long before it started charging. For a subscription site, that level of trust is vital. People need to know who you are before you can ask them to start paying a subscription fee.

Branding

Building a brand is more of an art than a science. Successful brands have understood the messages they want to communicate and the tools that they want to use to broadcast those messages. It's a process that takes time, but one that should end with the customer recognizing the seller's name and understanding that the company is reliable and trustworthy.

There have always been many different ways of creating that brand, from design to advertising and now viral advertising. But the

Figure 8.10 Tony Hsieh of Zappos uses Twitter to create a personal brand and connect with customers.

Web has now made it possible for individuals to create their own personal brands and use them to build their businesses.

ZAPPOS

Sure, there are personal brands that are bigger than that of Tony Hsieh, CEO of Zappos.com (www.zappos.com). Any story about Steve Jobs sends tech stocks flying across Nasdaq. Richard Branson, the founder of Virgin Group, has tried to balloon around the world to attract attention to his brand. But they're both old school. Tony Hsieh has helped to turn his online footwear and clothing store into a multi-million-dollar business in part by building his personal brand on the Web.

One way in which he has done that is through Twitter (Figure 8.10). Tony's Twitter background is all about the site, but his timeline is packed with inspirational quotes as well as information about his life. It's just one part of the company's branding, but it's helped to build a relationship with his customers so strong that in November 2009, Amazon bought the company in an $847 million stock buyout.

Coaching

Coaching usually involves a personal connection between seller and buyer. That means you have to find the channel that makes you most comfortable. Phone consultations are always simple, but webinars can work, classroom settings can bring in lots of people at the same time, and giant workshops can cram a year's income into one weekend. As long as you have the information and an audience eager to learn that information, your coaching method is up to you.

JACK THE GARDEN COACH

Most coaches sell information that will help their audiences make money. That makes sense. It's always easier to demonstrate the value of your knowledge when the audience can estimate how much they

Figure 8.11   Jack McKinnon teaches people to garden. It's not a moneymaking thing. It's a fun thing.

can earn once they know it. But it is possible to sell information that's just fun to know. Jack McKinnon is a gardening coach. He's been a professional gardener for 35 years; he writes about gardening and also coaches private gardeners in the Bay Area. His web site JacktheGardenCoach.com (www.jackthegardencoach.com) simply explains who he is, what he does, and invites people to drop him a line to book him for a two-hour consultation in their garden (Figure 8.11).

There are news items and links to his gardening articles that help to build trust, and Jack is also planning to offer downloads of his gardening tips, a smart way to use information products to create an audience. But the coaching itself couldn't be more enjoyable for him: He visits clients, walks around in their garden for a couple of hours, and tells them what they can do to make their garden better. Simple.

Conclusion

When James Ritty, an Ohio saloon owner, created the first cash register in 1879, his motives were pretty simple. He wanted to stop his employees from stealing his takings. His machine, based on a device that counted the number of revolutions a ship's propeller made, kept track of his business's sales. Later versions included a drawer for the money. Putting a bell on that drawer meant that he also knew when his employees were handling the cash.

Registers have changed a bit since then. They're now digital, programmable, and can even track the purchasing patterns of individual customers, enabling the seller to make personalized special offers. They're more likely to take credit cards than cash, and now that Jack Dorsey, the brains behind Twitter, has invented Square, a small credit card reader that plugs into the earphone socket of an iPhone, they can even fit in your pocket.

But they no longer go KaChing.

That's a shame, because to entrepreneurs, it's a wonderful sound. Each ring is an endorsement, a reminder that all of their hard work has been done for a reason. They've had the idea; they've implemented the idea; and now they're getting their reward.

This book hasn't made a KaChing sound, either. But it has given you the means to make deals and take cash.

For anyone with a head for business and a mind to be his own boss, the Internet represents an open country of unlimited opportunity. Mining that opportunity will take effort. Once your passive revenue systems are in place you'll be able to relax—a little—but it will take time and solid work to put those structures in place.

The good news is that the structures now come almost prefabricated. If once building an Internet site meant poring over code and tracking down bugs in the HTML, today's Web publishers can buy templates off the shelf. It's as though the Wild West were still out there, but instead of heading out into the wilderness with a tin plate and a lot of dreams, you get to choose your patch. . .then build your own town by dropping in the proven businesses you want to run.

Of course, you still have to bring people into the town. You have to offer services and products that people want to buy. You need to create a brand so that visitors know what they're getting when they pass through, then persuade them to stick around because they like it. That's work, but it's work that's available to anyone willing to do it.

The Internet provides all the opportunity that anyone could wish for and makes it available at a price that's incredibly low. When you can create an ad-supported web site, in minutes, for free, you won't be able to find an opportunity with lower entry requirements—or higher potential.

In this book, I've described the most important models that I've used to build my seven-figure Internet business.

I started by pointing out the size of the Internet's opportunity. That you no longer need to be a geek, a programmer, or even possess any technical knowledge at all to become an Internet publisher means that the Internet's opportunities are now available to anyone. That's an incredible thing.

I then talked about what you will need to be a success online: You'll need to be you. I explained how everyone has unique knowledge, and why that unique knowledge (whether it comes from the workplace or from the things you love to do in your spare time) has value. The Internet lets you cash in on that value.

Usually that's done by creating content, and in Chapter 3, I discussed seven types of content that you can create and almost a dozen different ways of monetizing that content through advertising.

Web content is free; information products cost money, often lots of money. The source of the information is the same. You're still telling people what you know about your job or your hobby, but you're doing it in more detail than a web site allows . . . and charging a price much closer to the true value of that knowledge. Nor is it particularly difficult to create, sell, and deliver those products. You can even buy a shopping cart off the shelf these days.

When you sell your information products, you'll be relying on affiliates, independent resellers who earn a commission for every sale. That's an opportunity that you can take up as well. Much though depends on the connection that you manage to build with your audience. Whenever you're selling online, you have to guide your market through a four-step sales process that takes leads from knowing you and liking you to trusting you and paying you. That's particularly true of affiliate products, which work best when the links are delivered in the text as part of a personal recommendation.

Affiliate sales have to be made again and again. Subscription fees to membership sites are renewed automatically, provided you can deliver services and products of high enough quality to attract subscribers and keep them on board. In Chapter 6, I revealed the ingredients of a successful membership site and explained how you can build one.

Finally, when your brand is strong enough and your community's trust in you is deep enough, you can even offer personal coaching, a wonderfully rewarding way to sell your knowledge and help people achieve their dreams.

Over the years, as Internet marketing has grown and matured, it's developed ready-made systems that anyone can use and profit from. It's not a cash register; it's a cash machine, one that's free for anyone to own and master.

It might not make the kind of KaChing sound you could once hear in stores across the country, but it is a business, and you can operate it.

As a thank-you to readers of this book, I am making a one-of-a-kind KaChing Button available to you for free! Just like the button pictured on the cover, this green button with the dollar sign makes the KaChing sound when pushed. I ask only that you include a nominal fee to cover the shipping and handling of your button.

To get your own KaChing Button now, visit www.KaChing Button.com/get/.

May you create an online business that pays and pays, with more than enough KaChing to go around.

Other books by Joel Comm

Twitter Power: How to Dominate Your Market One Tweet at a Time

www.TwitterPower.com

Social media is here to stay, and one of the most powerful social media sites to emerge in recent years is Twitter. In this insightful and entertaining book, Joel Comm tells you why you should be using Twitter to market yourself or your business, and the best ways to do so. Don't get left behind the social media curve! If you've heard a lot about Twitter but are wondering how to go about actually using it, this book will show you the way. And if you're already on Twitter and are wondering what all the fuss is about, *Twitter Power* will illuminate new tips and tricks for you to try.

The AdSense Code

www.TheAdSenseCode.com

The definitive guide to making money with Google's AdSense program for site publishers, this 230-page book provides the strategies and techniques used to generate passive income with any content-based Web site. A New York Times bestseller, Comm's easy-to-read-and-apply instructions have been applauded by thousands of readers. The hands-on solutions address the concerns and challenges faced by content publishers in their quest to attract targeted traffic, improve content relevance, and increase revenue streams. The world's recognized expert on Google AdSense, Joel Comm provides you with the keys you need to "crack" the AdSense Code and unlock the secrets to making money online. (ISBN 1933596708)

Click Here to Order: Stories of the World's Most Successful Internet Marketing Entrepreneurs

www.ClickHereToOrderBook.com

Most people associate being an Internet millionaire with the dotcom craze of the late 1990s. But a small band of Internet marketing pioneers were quietly making their fortune before anyone googled the term "making money online." *Click Here to Order* shows how ordinary people became Internet millionaires by applying their skills, talent, and passion to the Internet. Learn the history of the Internet from the 1960s to the present day, and be inspired by the stories of those who paved the way for the rest of us. Features stories of legendary Internet marketing figures such as Mark Joyner, Armand Morin, John Reese, Yanik Silver, Jeff Walker, and many more! (ISBN 1600371736)

Index